Minnesota in the Mail

Minnesota
in the Mail

Bonnie G. Wilson

A POSTCARD ★ HISTORY ★

 MINNESOTA HISTORICAL SOCIETY PRESS

www.mnhs.org/mhspress

The Minnesota Historical Society Press is a member of the Association of American University Presses.

Book design by Wesley B. Tanner/Passim Editions, Ann Arbor

Manufactured in China by Pettit Network, Inc., Afton, Minnesota

10 9 8 7 6 5 4 3 2 1

∞ This book is printed on a coated paper manufactured on an acid-free base to ensure a long life.

International Standard Book Number 0-87351-481-5 (cloth)

Library of Congress Cataloging-in-Publication Data
Wilson, Bonnie G. 1945–
Minnesota in the mail : a postcard history / Bonnie G. Wilson.
p. cm.
Includes index.
ISBN 0-87351-481-5 (alk. paper)
1. Minnesota—History—Pictorial works. 2. Postcards—Minnesota.
I. Title.

F607.W555 2004   2003019835

Credits
Patterns A and B, page 15: photos by Midge Bolt
"Greetings from St. Paul," page 27: collection of Robert Ott
"Wonderland," page 78: collection of Deborah Swanson
"Peterson family" and "Photographer's Studio Register," page 86: Gust Akerlund Collection, Cokato Historical Society
"Postman in car," page 93, and "Wilson family," page 95: author's collection
All other images are from Minnesota Historical Society collections.

Minnesota in the Mail

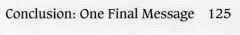

To Dean, Nina, and Annika Wilson

Preface & Acknowledgments

ostcards are survivors. Beautiful and evocative, they live on in drawers, scrapbooks, and collectors' cabinets for decades after being printed and sold. They also endure as a communication medium, useful and thriving more than one hundred years after their invention. Today we encounter postcards in museum shops, at food and fuel stops, and at tourist attractions. We receive them daily as mailed advertisements. We send them electronically. And the word "postcard" still functions linguistically to connote a certain kind of scene: picture-perfect.

Postcards from all eras inspire positive associations, reminding us of places, friends, relatives, vacations, and staying in touch. They also evoke history. On the surface, of course, they depict how things looked at some moment in time. Additionally, the postcard—an object created by a commercial industry—has its own history, some of which is highlighted in this book. It is remarkable how many clues to its past a postcard displays: trademarks, makers' names, format, postmarks, captions, messages, signatures, and addresses. Each mark relates to a piece of our past: business, technology, transport, communication, and travel. Upon closer inspection, one realizes that a postcard is more than just a pretty picture.

I have had the pleasure of collecting postcards for the Minnesota Historical Society since 1972. Many come to me unsolicited, arriving direct from storerooms and attics after a cleaning binge. I am always eager to open these

packages to see a new town or site that was invisible to me until that moment. Postcards show scenes that have disappeared: tiny towns, mom-and-pop resorts, roadside eateries, modest motels, and startling disasters that were visually recorded by no one outside the postcard industry.

To better understand the wonderful world of postcard collecting, I began a collection for myself. Many enthusiasts start with their hometown, but since mine is St. Paul, a place I had already seen a hundred times over in the collection, I decided to acquire cards of my summer vacation spots around Petoskey, Michigan. I found an old camera store in nearby East Jordan that hadn't sold all of its Petoskey cards from the 1940s, providing me with a beginner set of views from one time period. Then I spent leisurely summer hours at northern Michigan antique shops and fairs acquiring earlier views. More recently I've made regular visits to eBay, the on-line auction site, to see what else is available on my other "hometown."

To complete the research for this book, I examined more than twenty thousand postcards in the Minnesota Historical Society collections. I read the captions on all of them, glimpsing the lives and travels of hundreds of Minnesotans over the years. I found I was drawn to certain images—whether they were made during the golden age, the linen era, or much later—usually cards that show the finest printing and most eye-catching scenes. Over the course of my research, I also visited postcard enthusiasts

to explore the depths of their collections. When a collector concentrates on one place for many years, he or she accumulates an amazing number of cards and a thorough knowledge of the local makers. Finally, I interviewed contemporary postcard publishers in Minnesota to get a better idea of how the industry operates.

View cards—those that show scenes and places—are the focus of this book. Minnesota has been depicted on postcards in a variety of ways over the years, communicating what was deemed important in different eras. Comparing postcard views of a town taken seventy years apart illustrates not only how the town has physically changed but also how postcard consumers prefer to remember the site at a particular time. A postcard has both a maker and a buyer, each with an idea of what best represents a place.

In order to really appreciate postcards, the viewer should understand the origins of the object and who played a role in its creation, distribution, and use. As an aid to readers—of this book and of postcards more generally—the first section is a primer, introducing the many facets of a postcard. The four sections following the primer exemplify the main functions that postcards serve. "My Hometown" includes cards from around the state of Minnesota, each created to show off a town's unique and interesting features, selected to demonstrate how these categories were defined and redefined as time passed. "Our Business" contains cards that illustrate commerce and la-

bor, many functioning to promote and advertise. "The Personals" represents the work of amateur and commercial photographers during a thirty-year period when real-photo postcards were commonly made of family, friends, workplaces, and homes to communicate a personal message to a select few. The final section, "Our Vacation," illustrates the primary function of postcards in the second half of the twentieth century: to promote tourist sites and to inform the folks back home that we are visiting a wonderful place.

Having observed people's obvious pleasure as they browse through piles of postcards in an antique store or their grandmother's cabinet, I wanted to escort armchair travelers through the visual delights of Minnesota's postcards over the last century. I hope you enjoy the trip.

Acknowledgments

I acknowledge the following people for their help and information:

Shannon M. Pennefeather, for her kind and intelligent editing; Gary Pearson, Dick Schalow, Larry Erickson, Jerry Stransky, and Earl Fisher for their helpful interviews; James Fogerty, Jean Brookins, Elaine Carte, and Phil Freshman for their support and encouragement; Ann-Marie Rose, Sharon Bartels, and Richard Fisch for their immense help with understanding the printing process; Mick Caouette, John Dougherty, Harold Zosel, Dr. Robert Becker, and Alissa Rosenberg for research assistance; and the Charles E. Flandrau Research Leave Fund for sabbatical support.

I am grateful to these individuals and organizations for assistance with caption information:

William Morris; John Cole; Shawn Hewitt; Richard Ferrell; Ben Thoma; Karen Cooper; Jim Johnson; Terry Lindow; Dennis Wright; Steve Krahn; Aaron Isaacs; Rick Weigand; Judy Lawrence; A. J. Nickaboine; Virginia Sam; George Nelson; Tom Cox; Mark Haidet; Kate Roberts; Linda McShannock; Scott Anfinson; Skip Drake; Duane Swanson; Deborah Swanson; Charles Nelson; Tom Amble; Marcia Anderson; Patricia Maus, Northeast Minnesota Historical Center; Dona Brown, Meeker County Historical Society; Michael Worcester, Cokato Historical Society; Char Henn, Goodhue County Historical Society; Ann Lundberg, Big Stone County Historical Society; Jo Mihelich and Lois Johnson, Waconia Heritage Association; Jon Velishek, Rice County Historical Society; Pat Zankman, Cook County Historical Society; Marion Shilgren, Museum of Mining; Winona County Historical Society; Stearns County Historical Society; Beltrami County Historical Society; State Historical Society of Wisconsin; and the Curt Teich Postcard Archives at the Lake County Discovery Museum, Wauconda, Illinois.

Postcards for sale in Charles L. Merryman's photography studio, Kerkhoven, Minnesota, 1903

The Postcard Primer

Some Postcard Basics

The Germans thought of it first. A simple way to communicate, a way that saved money and time: offer a small card on which people could write short personal or business messages instead of having to compose a long letter. The problem, according to the idea's originator, was that letters had become filled with unnecessary words and cost too much to send. Heinrich von Stephan, a German postal official, proposed the new "open post sheet" to the Austro-German Postal Conference in 1865. The German states thought it a worthy idea, but they couldn't agree among themselves as to whether their several governments would make or lose money on the proposition, so it passed to the Austrians to introduce the first official postcard in 1869. Suggested by Emanuel Herrmann, professor of political economy, the card was eagerly adopted by most European countries within a few years.

The U.S. Post Office introduced the penny postcard in 1873, tightly controlling its issuance by allowing only U.S. government–printed cards to travel for one cent. Non-government-issued cards cost two cents to send, the same rate as an envelope. Anyone could print business messages or greetings on one side, but the cards had to be printed by and purchased from the U.S. Post Office if they were to travel at the cheaper rate. These early American cards usually carried business advertising—preprinted text and the occasional line engraving. Illustrations were not on every card.

GOVERNMENT BUILDING.

OFFICIAL SOUVENIR POSTAL

WORLD'S COLUMBIAN EXPOSITION

**Official Souvenir Postal,
World's Columbian Exposition**

*One of the first color views distributed in the
United States, this card from the 1893 World's
Columbian Exposition in Chicago shows the
fair's administration building.*

The first American mass-produced, color-illustrated postcards appeared in 1893 at the World's Columbian Exposition in Chicago. Delicate color lithographs of the exposition buildings, they marked the beginning of a new visual era. Prior to this time, all mass-produced photographs were black and white and most magazine illustrations were line engravings rendered in black and white. Color was available on chromolithographic prints, like those of Currier and Ives, and in paintings. Purchasing and sharing an inexpensive color view was a new and exciting experience. Although the earliest American postcards still resembled color drawings, the technology soon transformed them into color views that looked like real color photographs, a medium still in its infancy.

There soon followed a "golden age" of postcards. From about 1905 to 1915, postcards were published and sent by the billions. In 1907, one German printer alone made an estimated 120 million cards. Examination of any large collection shows that most cards were produced and mailed during this period, making it a golden age for research as well

as for collecting. One measure of the intensity is the number of postcards traveling by mail. In Minneapolis, a 1905 newspaper article exclaimed, "A conservative estimate places the number of cards that will pass thru the city mails during Christmas week at 120,000." American retail postcard sales, another measure of success, passed $50 million a year in 1909, according to *Picture Postcards in the United States, 1893–1918,* by Dorothy Ryan. The St. Paul paper reported in January 1908, "Postcarditis has St. Paul within its grasp and has every evidence of becoming chronic." According to the article, one dealer at a hotel often sold five or six dozen views to a single customer. Another dealer reported selling one hundred thousand cards in one month.

Not simply a golden age of quantity, it was also a golden age of quality, with absolutely gorgeous color cards printed in Germany, England, and the United States. Collections often center on this era and postcard books usually feature it, largely because the cards were so beautifully printed and abundantly available.

This golden age was powered by events and technologies that together produced immense popularity. The halftone screen came into wide use in the 1890s, allowing any photograph to be broken up into small dots for inking on a press. Rural free delivery, established in 1896, increased the range of postcard distribution just at the time when travel was increasing. Typical travelers were anxious to send home news of their safe arrival and a scene of their most recent stopping place. And in 1898, the U.S. government released its monopoly on printing postcards and opened up a new source of income for printers and small publishing businesses.

There are two basic types of postcards: real-photo cards printed one by one in a darkroom, and press-printed cards made by the thousands. The real-photo cards are everyman's card. After Kodak brought out preprinted "post card" photo paper in 1902, anyone could make postcards in a home darkroom or photographer's studio. Real-photo cards appear in family albums as black-and-white portraits of ancestors or in antique stores as black-and-white images of small-town main streets.

The press-printed cards were a bigger deal. More had to be produced, usually at least three thousand, in order to make the pressrun worthwhile. Typically these cards show scenes of larger towns or landmark buildings. As attested to on the back of most early printed cards, the Germans did the majority of the printing until about 1910.

The standard look of the printed card has changed over the years, and the viewer may place a card in history by examining its physical features. The very earliest view cards were generally composites, with one or more scenes surrounding the writing space on the front of the card.

Soon the view grew larger, covering all of the card's face save a small white space for writing. In 1907 post offices began allowing messages to be composed on the back, and the fronts of cards became borderless, allowing a full view of compelling scenes and the printer's art. Then, around 1915, printers introduced a white border, probably to save ink, and created a look that continued into the 1930s. During that decade a new textured surface and brighter colors appeared, launching what many collectors describe as the "linen era" of 1930 to 1945. A final change emerged in 1939, when "chrome" cards were developed. Chromes are color photographs printed with four half-tone screens made from color transparencies. They look like a color photograph, but a magnifying glass reveals small dots of four colors. Chromes dominated postcard printing after 1950 and are standard fare at today's tourist stops. For examples of the evolving process, see pages 7, 8, and 9.

Anatomy of a Postcard

Postcards offer pathways into history, stimulating questions and providing answers. Looking closely at a card, viewers focus first on the scene, then perhaps on the message. Next, they might wonder about the very small print that names the publisher, photographer, or printer. The postmark and stamp provide further clues about the life of the card, while its preprinted caption may answer some questions but raise others. All of these elements make the modest postcard a multifaceted object with links to the imagery, technology, and customs of the time in which it was produced.

The Postcard View of the World:
The Picture Carries a Message

When we choose a postcard to send, our selection says something about our aesthetic taste, our mood, or the sights we find interesting. But postcards don't allow us to send the exact image we may wish to because they don't show everything. Our choices are limited to what is emphasized during a particular era. In Minnesota, the postcard view of the state falls within three broad periods: civic pride and hometown views, 1900–1920; tourism and tourist spots, 1920–1960; and shorthand abstractions of place, 1960–present. Of course, all eras retain or predict elements of earlier or later ones, but within each is a predominant theme.

During the golden age of postcards, almost every town with a name had a card to represent it. Collectors who focus on a town or region will find the majority of their views date to this era. But even with this geographical richness there are limitations. If the collector wants a bird's-eye view or a shot of main street, he will most likely find one. Harder to locate are images of the homes and

St. Paul, Minn.

Paul Reichelt's first published postcard, a multiview similar to German Grüss Aus cards, was composed of representative images of St. Paul, Minnesota, in one corner and writing space at the bottom.

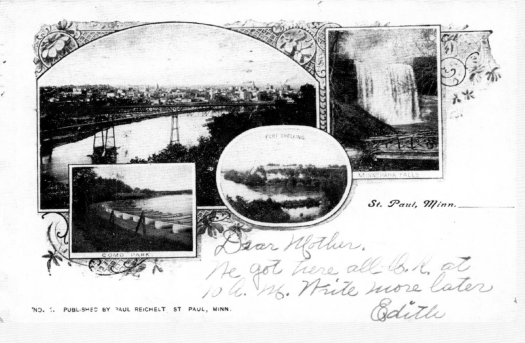

Duluth Yacht Club

Its undivided back reserved for the address, this pre-1907 card required the sender to squeeze a succinct message next to an image of the Duluth Yacht Club.

GIRLS WANTED, MINNEAPOLIS, MINN.

**Girls Wanted,
Minneapolis, Minn.**

A post-1907 borderless card, published by V. O. Hammon, advertises suitable men canoeing in Minneapolis.

**Rustic Lounge, Grand View Lodge,
on Gull Lake near Brainerd**

A white-border card mailed in 1929 and published by the Duluth Photo Engraving Company promotes the eclectic and rustic lounge at Grand View Lodge near Brainerd.

RUSTIC LOUNGE, GRAND VIEW LODGE, ON GULL LAKE, NEAR BRAINERD, P. O. NISSWA, MINN.   796-29

M-92—Streamliner Crossing Mississippi River over Stone Arch Bridge, Minneapolis, Minn.

Streamliner Crossing Mississippi River over Stone Arch Bridge, Minneapolis, Minn.

A linen-era card by Curt Teich illustrates Minneapolis's modernity, a sleek streamliner crossing the historic Stone Arch Bridge with the cityscape filling the background. Many white-border linen cards were produced during this period as well.

Chamber of Commerce, International Falls

This chrome card published for City Drug Store in International Falls features the chamber of commerce with arrows and fish pointing the way to myriad tourist destinations.

residential districts of both rural and urban communities, the private areas of town. In general, postcards emphasized the town and not the countryside, and this is true even in Minnesota, despite its strong rural economy. The popularity of hometown views, especially of main streets, coincides with the city beautiful movement and reflects the enthusiastic civic boosterism depicted by novelists like Sinclair Lewis. Townspeople sold cards reflecting their pride—usually the business district—and passers-through chose images that represented their journeys to towns.

Around 1920, another era in Minnesota postcard history began to emerge. As tourism developed in the state, the postcard industry refocused its attention, seeking a new and sustainable market. Tourism originated in the form of roadside camps and farmhouse accommodations for the occasional hunting or fishing group, but soon local independent resort owners established businesses around the state's famously multitudinous lakes. Whereas earlier postcard consumers arrived by train at the town depot, they now arrived by car at the resort and were primed to write home about the big fish or the restful lake. They cared less about sending pictures of main street, choosing instead to advertise the cozy accommodations or the tree-filled scenery. When passing through town, they received advertising cards from motels or restaurants, eliminating a stop at the main street drugstore to purchase a town view.

Tourism was a boon to the postcard industry until the 1950s, when card production contracted. Hometown and resort cards became things of the past as generic postcards, showing no place in particular and every place in general, began to predominate. Today few cards exhibit images of specific places, and many symbolize and abstract a place. If a small town is represented at all, it is by an aerial view, seldom a main street. If a city is pictured, the view usually features a skyline or major attraction. Statues and roadside sculptures of giant fish or incredible creatures have muscled in to represent Minnesota towns. Wildlife imagery simultaneously embodies a specific town and the entire state, as today Minnesotans are represented by moose, cows, raccoons, chipmunks, wolves, foxes, bear, deer, and a variety of birds. We no longer portray ourselves as proud builders of rural towns or cozy resorts.

This evolution of postcard imagery is replicated in other states and is not unique to Minnesota. Some might consider it a pattern of decline, but it is in fact a reflection of market trends, determined in large part by the postcard consumer.

The Back Side of the Postcard: A Message to the World

"Arrived safely, will write more later," is the quintessential postcard message, more common than "having a wonder-

ful time, wish you were here." Both messages convey the desire to touch base, assuring the recipient of the writer's well-being somewhere in the world and offering a promise or wish to make the reader feel good, too. The most typical Minnesota messages are weather reports, brief travelogues, and updates to family members from those who are away from home.

It comes as no surprise that the most common postcard topic is the weather. Since the state is notorious for its nasty and variable conditions, messages from Minnesota naturally have much to say on the subject. There are often benign and complimentary weather reports, but these do not stimulate the imagination. It is the extremes that draw our attention: "We had an awful storm today, blew both chimneys off our building and broke a window in Mrs. Van's room. Broke all the windows in the Catholic Church. Was fierce" (Frazee, April 7, 1909). Some writers even use the weather as an excuse for sending a postcard instead of a letter: "Too hot to write—93 in the shade most every day" (July 18, 1910). And every transplant to Minnesota will recognize the fear expressed in this message: "I very nearly passed out of existence last week the day it was two below and the folks here are wondering what I will do when it is twenty five below" (New Ulm, January 23, 1908). Scaring newcomers with dire weather predictions is a popular form of entertainment for Minnesotans.

Besides its weather, Minnesota is also known for its vast assemblage of sparkling bodies of water. From a land of ten thousand lakes, people predictably send thousands of vacation and travel reports. In the early part of the twentieth century, the messages described a leisurely pace, but as the automobile overtook the railroad as the preferred form of transportation to the lakes and across the state, the messages themselves picked up a sense of speed, almost frenzy, until they became touch-and-go lists of mileage totals and places seen. An example of the former, "Zippy" wrote in August 1909 from her vacation retreat in Frontenac to her friend Vera: "We lie in hammocks all day long, sleep, eat, read, play a little bridge, and go on as short walks as I can persuade them to take. The vegetative life for fair. It is grand to have our own cottage—in the evening it is possible to don the most negligent of negligees and sit on our own little porch." Compare that scene to the 1950 travel report sent from International Falls: "Saw the folks at 3 Lakes and then drove to Virginia, Minn. Up at 6, and have come 100 for breakfast here. Then on as far as we can get into North Dakota." By mid-century, there is no time for languid days and nights at the lake.

Reporting on work rather than play, many golden age postcards were sent by schoolteachers newly arrived at their posts. After settling in Hutchinson, Beth wrote to

her friend Jeannie in Minneapolis three days in a row, September 9–11, 1907. At first she exclaimed, "Everything here is ideal. I have a fine boarding place, pleasant room and like teaching. The children here are clean and bright. I will write you soon. With love to all, Beth." The next day brought this missive: "We are having cold dreary weather here, My school work keeps me busy most of the time. They have a fine minister here and such cultured people. In this town there are thirteen churches and only four saloons. Isn't that good? With love, Beth." By the third day, her enthusiasm had dimmed a bit: "Tonight I go to a reception for the teachers given at the ME church. This is a quiet peaceful place and one can get well rested here. I know it will do me good. Give my love to the family. As ever Beth." In this case we sense the excitement of a new arrival at the beginning of her career, her passion quickly fading with the onset of reality in main-street America.

Reading postcard messages momentarily brings the reader into the mind of the writer, even if the writer is an inhabitant of the past. A brief epistle can be evocative of another life, another time. Early critics of the newly invented postcard worried that it would open the mail to voyeurs, and in fact it has, as many of us pause to read the cards we find in drawers and antique shops and take a moment to imagine ourselves in the writer's world.

Postcard Photographers: The First to Make Their Mark

All view cards are based on photographs, either real or transformed. In small towns during the golden age, main street photographers—men like Gust Akerlund of Cokato and Charles Merryman of Kerkhoven—made photos in their darkrooms, printing street scenes onto photosensitive postcard paper. Larger companies like the Bloom Brothers of Minneapolis or A. C. Bosselman of New York bought pictures from big commercial studios like Sweet of Minneapolis or Ingersoll of St. Paul and sent them to printers in Germany or elsewhere. During the golden age, photographers' names often appeared on the front of postcards, but after the boom their names disappeared until the 1960s, when it again became common practice to credit the photographer.

Postcard photographers do not set out to document the world's main streets and vacation spots. They take pictures of scenes that sell. By their very nature the views are selective and sanitized. Nevertheless, these photographers have recorded thousands of scenes—particularly of rural towns and small commercial endeavors like motels and restaurants—that would otherwise have passed unrecorded by the camera.

The Publisher Makes His Mark:
The System's Middleman

A central component of the postcard business, the postcard publisher studies the market, selects the photographs, hires the printer, sells the cards to drugstores, variety stores, and convenience stores, and keeps the racks stocked. Minnesota has been home to about fifty-five postcard publishers over the years. Many publishers are represented by design logos, like the sailboat for V. O. Hammon, while others simply print their name on the card.

It appears that Paul Reichelt of St. Paul was the first Minnesotan to publish postcards. He issued a set of four black-and-white lithographed cards from his bookstore in St. Paul around 1898. They each carried multiple views of St. Paul formatted much like the European *Grüss Aus* (greetings from) postcards.

In 1905 a trade magazine reported, "the demand for illustrated postal cards is daily assuming larger proportions and there are no prospects of the slightest abatement anywhere in sight." Into this active economic environment plunged the majority of Minnesota postcard businesses: twenty-seven different St. Paul and Minneapolis companies entered the postcard publishing frenzy between 1907 and 1912. Most stayed in the business for only one or two years during this volatile, experimental period, but a few companies continued with it for the long term. Adolf Pearson and the Bloom Brothers, Harry, Benjamin, and Moses, of Minneapolis successfully operated postcard businesses for several decades. Their names appear on hundreds of Minnesota views, and they deserve much credit for recording Minnesota's early-twentieth-century urban and village environments.

The majority of golden age postcard companies, whether national or local, did not survive as postcard publishers past the 1920s. According to postcard historian George Miller, 1909 marked the beginning of the downward trend. Among the many contributing factors was a protective tariff placed on postcards that year by the Payne-Aldrich Act, meant to stimulate the American postcard business by increasing the tariff on cards printed in Germany, which had dominated the market until then. However, before the tariff went into effect, jobbers and importers bought and distributed all the German cards they possibly could, thereby overloading the market and producing a glut. Prices plummeted, sometimes from as much as two for a nickel to ten for a nickel. The final poke in the postcard balloon came from the introduction, in 1912, of folded greeting cards, which soon replaced the postcard greetings that had been a major part of the industry.

As small businesses, postcard publishers depend on

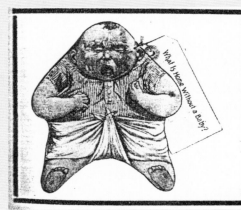
Advertisement,
R. Steinman & Co., St. Paul, Minn.

Richard Steinman advertised his postcards and novelties in the Northwestern Druggist.

diversification for survival. Many have sold novelties as well as postcards, from the golden age up through today. Richard Steinman advertised felt pennants and cry-baby dolls along with his line of cards, while Bloom Brothers specialized in leather souvenirs. The Wright, Barrett, and Stillwell Company of St. Paul sold stationery and roofing materials, publishing postcards on the side. Some mid-century publishers were news agents, distributing newspapers and magazines as well as postcards.

To ensure their success, postcard publishers have always relied on person-to-person sales. Arriving on Main Street from the nearby depot, they approached the local druggist or variety store owner with samples of the latest in views. If the company sold real-photo cards, like the Co-Mo or A. Pearson Companies, the salesman was also the photographer, offering the views he took on his last trip into town or asking the store owner what he would like

photographed. After taking orders, he boarded the next train and canvassed the next town, eventually returning to the Twin Cities to fill the orders and begin all over again. In subsequent decades, the mode of transport changed: salesmen from NMN and W. A. Fisher traveled the roads of northern Minnesota and sold postcards out of their cars or vans. The key to maintaining a successful postcard business was personal contact, but mail-order and catalogue sales became common at the close of the twentieth century.

To sustain local connections, the postcard publisher allied his business to drugstores and variety stores by placing the owner's name on the card as a sponsor or distributor. The local business did not actually carry out the publishing activities described above; the owners merely put in an order and approved the views. But being named on the card was a subtle form of advertising, so to in-

crease sales the real publisher stepped aside and sometimes did not receive credit on the card.

The postcard publishing business is often family-run, transferring from one generation to the next. An example is the A. Pearson Company, begun by Adolf and Theodore Pearson, brothers from Sweden. Adolf passed on the business to his son, Everett. Similarly, NMN owners Dick and Ella Schalow will be succeeded by their son.

Most publishers agree that the common elements of the postcard publishing business—diversification, personal contact, and local ownership—have not changed over the years, whereas the appearance and manufacturing method of the cards has changed greatly.

Postcard Production: The Mark of the Printer

A postcard printer's mark is an array of dots. Because postcards look so photographic, it is easy to forget that all but real-photo cards are products of a printing press. A magnifying glass placed on a postcard will show its difference from a photograph: a pattern of black-and-white or colored dots arrayed evenly, as in illustrations A and B. If magnification reveals four colors arranged in "rosettes," as in illustration B, the card is a chrome printed after 1940. Photographs, including all real-photo postcards, have a continuous tone silver surface and show no pattern whatsoever.

A. Dot pattern of a screened image

B. Rosette pattern appearing on all chrome postcards

The earliest view cards were printed lithographically, the view transferred onto a lithographic stone. However, most view postcards through the 1950s were printed on a lithographic press using a half-tone screen that broke up the original black-and-white photographic image into the dot pattern. (As printer Earl Fisher said during an interview, "The image has to be screened. You break it up into fine dots; otherwise you just come out with a blob of ink.") A lithographic press uses a rolled metal plate to lay down the dots. It works on the principle that water and

greasy ink don't mix. Ink is applied to the printing plate and adheres to its tacky surface whereas water, sprayed onto the paper, repels the ink and leaves white spaces. To create the illusion of color, the card is run through a press several times, using different plates for each color. The more colors seen under magnification, the more times the card passed through the press. Some cards were printed in black and white and then tinted by hand, often very finely. The cheapest cards were printed in black and white and given a quick brush of one or two colors to suggest a blue sky or a bit of grass.

Germany was the leader in postcard printing until the tariff of 1909 and the onset of World War I signaled the demise of its prominence in the American marketplace. German printers like C. G. Roeder and Emil Pinkau kept their exact methods secret. In fact, they didn't even credit their companies on the back of the card, using only the generic "Made in Germany," forcing today's postcard researchers to do some sleuthing to determine which printer made which cards.

Midwestern companies like Curt Teich of Chicago took the lead in American postcard printing when the German presses were no longer economical options for U.S. publishers. The Curt Teich Company used huge offset presses to print millions of cards. Like virtually all postcard printers, Teich used the "gang run" method, in which different postcards for different customers were printed on the same sheet at the same time, minimizing costs to each publisher. Additionally, modern presses could print more than one color at a time, a technical improvement that enabled the printer to produce a large volume of cards for a low price. During Curt Teich's long history from 1898 to 1978, it printed for most of the major postcard publishers in Minnesota, including Bloom Brothers and Richard Steinman.

During the golden age of postcards, publisher Victor O. Hammon of Minneapolis and Chicago used a printer who created color by arraying the dots in a sort of rosette pattern distinctive to V. O. Hammon cards. It is not known who the printer was, but the method foreshadows the process of four-color printing seen on postcards made in the second half of the twentieth century.

A new type of card, based on a color transparency instead of a black-and-white photograph, appeared in 1939. Called a "chrome" because it begins with a Kodachrome or Ektachrome transparency, the card is made by applying four colors—yellow, cyan, magenta, and black—in a rosette pattern of dots that produces the illusion of all colors. The color image is printed on an offset press using four plates, each transferring the ink to a rubber blanket that then presses the ink onto the paper. This is the method used by the W. A. Fisher Company of Virginia, Minnesota, on their large Heidelberg press.

Heidelberg press

A printing press used by the W. A. Fisher Company to print postcards.

The first chrome cards to be mass-produced were scenes of the American West offered as giveaways by the Union Oil Company. By the 1960s, all cards were printed as chromes, and this remains so today. Before chromes were introduced, the color on postcards was fictional, suggested by the client, the publisher, or the art director in the printing plant and not necessarily representing the true scene. This detail is important to keep in mind when using cards as a primary source for historic preservation activities. And, with the newest development in postcard printing, digital imaging, the photographer or printer can enhance the image or change it drastically before it reaches the printing press, making even current views questionable historical documents.

Printing is the manufacturing aspect of postcard history. Over the last one hundred years, source and production changes have enabled the postcard to remain a viable commercial product.

Other Marksmen:
Linking the Postcard to Time and Place

The post office has always been influential in the postcard world. After cards were introduced in America in 1873, the postal service tightly controlled their issuance, allowing only government–printed cards to travel for one cent. But after restrictions eased in 1898, the postmark became the most obvious impression contributed by the U.S. Postal Service. Postmarks tell where the card began its journey and when. Before 1913, double cancellations sometimes indicated both the beginning and ending place and time, allowing officials to track the speediness of

their deliveries. Some cancellations are reminders of the railroad era: RPO, or "Railroad Post Office," marks appear on cards mailed from depots, trains, steamships, or streetcars. Instead of naming the town of origin, they designate the two ends of the line. Stamp cancellations are also marks of the postal system. Beginning with shapes and wavy lines and evolving to slogans like "Prevent Forest Fires" or occasions such as the state fair, cancellations prevent the reuse of stamps.

Contributing their own marks were makers of photographic paper for printing real-photo postcards. These businesses left a wide variety of trademarks on their products, preprinting their initials or product name in the area reserved for stamps. At first glance they seem to be words in a foreign language—"NOKO," "KRUXO," and "CYKO"—but they are simply trade names. Besides revealing who made the paper that the photographer bought, these strange words can be helpful in dating a real-photo card. For example, "CYKO" paper was produced between 1904 and the 1920s by the Ansco Company, while "DOPS" was produced for a much shorter time, 1937 to 1942. The book *Prairie Fires and Paper Moons: The American Photographic Postcard, 1900–1920* by Hal Morgan and Andreas Brown contains a useful chart for dating real-photo paper.

One final mark not to be overlooked by the historian is the caption preprinted on the back of the card. These breezy and somewhat unreliable statements are often written by the publisher, who bases his or her information on news bits and tourism brochures gathered along the way. Publishers don't have a lot of time for composition, which may account for the three different heights quoted on three different postcards of Minneapolis's landmark IDS building. Since the client is the chief concern, publishers may write whatever the client wants, factual or not. For this reason, postcard captions do not make good historical source material.

The basic lesson of this primer is that we can learn a great deal from postcards. We can learn about their makers and their senders, the business that created them and the system that got them through the mail. The advertisements, messages, logos, postmarks, and captions are all related to the creation and use of this object. As we "read" each of these marks, something that appears at first glance to be two-dimensional becomes multidimensional. All is not revealed on a single card, but the inquiring mind can use these clues to delve into the history of printing, publishing, commerce, and communication.

CHAPTER ONE

My Hometown

I have a dandy place here. Biwabik is a good town. We have two large school buildings, city hall, fire dept. paved streets and best of all nineteen good looking schoolma'ams.

Biwabik to Ely, September 22, 1909

Pleasure comes with seeing familiar faces and places, whether in family albums or in hometown postcard collections. We see best the scenes we recognize. Looking at a view of a town we've never experienced, we see a generic streetscape. Looking at our own town, we immediately recognize sites that elicit emotions and memories.

I remember the first time I saw old postcards of my hometown, St. Paul, Minnesota. Sitting on my mother's green brocade couch, I was trying desperately to illustrate my eighth grade history report on Minnesota. Then my mother appeared with a stack of old postcards, many of St. Paul in the first decade of the twentieth century. I was transfixed. "Where did these come from?" I quizzed her, con-

vinced I had seen the contents of every drawer and box in my house. "Grandma's things," she answered. Then I remembered that my grandfather had been a traveling minister in Minnesota. It seems that wherever he went, he sent postcards back to grandma, the backs covered with elaborate German script reporting on whom he had met and how he had slept. I shuffled through cards from Lakefield, Luverne, and Lester Prairie, finding them quaint but not intriguing. I had never been in those towns, so they all looked alike to me. But the ones from St. Paul: now those were something! Here was Como Park, a place I'd visited every Sunday since I could remember. But where were those Japanese Gardens and giant lily pads? Replaced by a golf course, I later learned. On a different card, I could recognize

the landscape of Indian Mounds Park, but the women in long skirts with the wicker baby buggy seemed like visitors from another planet. This mixture of the strange and the familiar drew me in, and I felt I had discovered history.

Postcard collectors submit to this same magnetic attraction. Most begin by seeking out images of their hometown, then of a few neighboring locales. Some go on to collect one view of every town in the state, even managing to find cards for tiny towns of fewer than fifty people. One collector whose goal is to represent every town in the state has views of eight hundred towns. He believes he could find as many as two thousand. For larger towns, populated by one to two thousand people, hundreds of cards can be found. A former mayor of Kenyon, Minnesota, population 1,600, has located more than three hundred cards of his town while another collector has catalogued over one thousand cards of St. Cloud. Neither is finished.

Without postcards, there would be little or no visual documentation of a majority of Minnesota towns during the first half of the twentieth century. Who would have made pictures of Hector or Lamberton if the postcard industry had not stimulated photographers to take to the streets and record some views? Whether by the hometown photographer or a traveling representative of a bigger company, photographs were made of virtually every town in Minnesota. Although not always acknowledged as post-

card views, they now illustrate every local history book published within the last thirty years.

A loss to visual history, the postcard picture of our hometown diminishes along with the industry over the years. Hometown postcard documentation is rich in the early period, 1905–15, less prevalent at midcentury, and hard to find after 1970. For example, the town of St. Cloud is represented by over 500 postcards before 1920, about 250 between 1920 and 1950, and only 100 or so chromes thereafter.

Postcard Patterns

The numerous cards available from the early part of the twentieth century reveal patterns in visual composition and subject matter. Because postcards are based on commerce—which images will turn a profit for publishers and salesmen—popular and successful views get repeated and patterns get established.

Postcard photographers adopted a few select points of view when depicting a town for its public. To capture the ever-popular "bird's-eye view," many a photographer climbed to the top of the grain elevator or the courthouse roof for a survey of what the proverbial bird sees. Or a view maker risked clashes with horse carts and automobiles by standing squarely in the main street intersection and pointing the lens down the central corridor at a van-

ishing triangle of businesses on either side of the street. Public buildings, schools, and churches were typically shot from a corner angle, exposing the architectural features of two sides instead of one. Photographic tradition and customer preference for the familiar dictated that this would be so. Visual innovation is seldom a factor in postcard photography.

As cultural artifacts, postcards emphasize certain aspects of one's hometown and obscure others. For example, the main street corridor is very important in the postcard view of small towns, but the individual business is not. Big city views, on the other hand, put less emphasis on the main streets and more on the skyline, the largest business buildings, and the parks.

Alison Isenberg, a scholar who has studied postcards of main streets, concluded that the main street corridor view, rather than the individual business building, was actually favored by small-town businessmen: "Most main street shops . . . preferred to 'advertise' themselves in postcards as a unified street front." They "promoted a street for transacting business, rather than touting the strengths of a particular store." She found that the popularity of hometown views coordinated with the city beautiful movement, along with boosterism and other aspects of civic pride.

Prior to World War I, city leaders nationwide were concerned with the beautification of their towns. Some hired planning consultants who would typically recommend simple improvements: bury unsightly utility wires, remove excess signage, improve sidewalks, and pave streets. Such suggestions involved major expenses for the city fathers but were no problem for postcard publishers, who served as visual housekeepers and handymen during the city beautiful era. Between the click of the camera's shutter and the drop of the card in the rack, views were frequently tidied up by the retouching pencil or the airbrush artist at the commercial printing plant. Curt Teich employed twenty artists to do the client's bidding, changing the messy realistic photo to match a town's "imagination of how their central business districts should have appeared," according to Isenberg. A case in point is Moorhead, Minnesota. In 1928, when residents were still striving to improve the look of their town, a postcard client sent a photograph to the Teich Company with instructions to take out the snow and large poles. By this time the artists were so accustomed to prettying up towns, they also paved the street, smoothed the sidewalk, and installed curbs.

Despite the focus on main street corridors, certain establishments did receive extra attention from the postcard industry. Hotels, banks, and grain elevators appear regularly in hometown postcard collections. Hotels used the postcards to advertise their business, and travelers found cards conveniently available for writing during a moment of rest. Celebrating the community more broadly, banks and grain elevators were symbols of prosperity. The elevators, those "cathedrals of the prairie," were the tallest structures in many small towns and naturally drew the camera's attention. And, occasionally postcards take us inside stores and businesses, where they provide a catalogue of cultural artifacts, revealed one by one as a magnifying glass travels over the view. Cases full of candy or cigars, postcards on a rack, fishing supplies on a counter: all are displayed from decades past.

After covering the business district, publishers looked to residential areas for views. Instead of selecting homes, however, they favored churches and schools, perhaps because the congregation, parents, and teachers were likely customers for the cards. Study of extensive hometown postcard collections reveals the dominant religions in particular towns, as those churches commissioned the most cards. St. Cloud, for example, one of the "largest enclaves of Catholics in the US," according to John Dominik Jr.'s bicentennial history, *Three Towns into One City: St. Cloud, Minnesota,* produced twice as many views of just two Catholic churches as it did of all the Protestant churches in the town. What's more, the Catholic churches appear on lithographically printed cards, indicating larger runs, while the Protestant churches are found on real-photo cards,

produced in smaller quantities. Harder to find are the homes and residential districts of both rural and urban communities. These were the private areas of town. Some homeowners did, however, commission real-photo cards of their castles.

A town's civic structures were not overlooked in postcard documentation: courthouses, post offices, and libraries appear frequently, although not as often as churches and schools. Similarly, natural beauty—whether a waterway or a park—drew the attention of postcard publishers of both town and city views. For Minneapolis and St. Paul, more than 25 percent of all cards show a park, water feature, or river. Other popular golden age categories include special events, like parades and speeches by dignitaries, and disasters, such as tornadoes and blizzards. But as newspapers printed more and more photographs to illustrate their stories, postcards ceased such reportage.

The Town Photographer

From 1900 to 1915, the source of many main street Minnesota views was the small-town photographer working in a tiny skylit studio, combining postcard work with portraiture to make a living. Sometimes he would serve as the town photojournalist, recording festivals and disasters. Typical of this small-town documentarian was Charles L. Merryman of Kerkhoven, Minnesota. He operated out of a

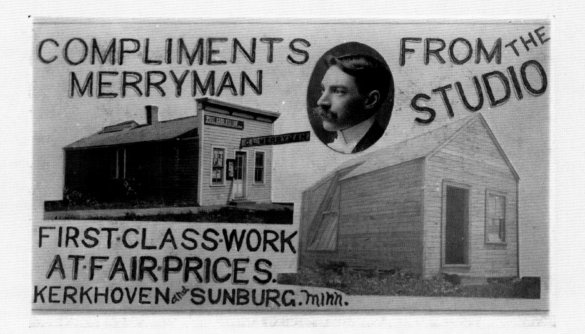

Compliments from the Merryman Studio

Charles L. Merryman printed real-photo postcards to advertise his two studios, in Kerkhoven and Sunburg, in 1910.

36-by-18-foot skylit studio for forty-seven years, making portraits and taking scenic pictures all over the county. During the golden age of postcards, he produced and sold both printed and real-photo views.

In St. Cloud, the outstanding real-photo card maker was Hugh Spencer, a druggist's son. Between 1906 and 1911, he made over one hundred views of St. Cloud, some of which were sent to lithography companies and made into printed cards in larger quantities. J. T. Austinson covered Kenyon, Minnesota, from 1903 to 1911, including the great April Fools' Day fire in 1911. Many of these arti-

sans disappeared from the photography scene after the postcard craze abated, but some refocused their business on portraiture and enjoyed lengthy careers.

The Itinerant Photo Postcard Business

After the golden years of postcard popularity, main street merchants had to rely on outsiders to depict their town. Many of the smallest towns were no longer portrayed on cards, but medium-sized Minnesota towns were documented by the A. Pearson Company of Minneapolis and the L. L. Cook Company of Milwaukee, Wisconsin. These

Genuine Photographs / Colored Post Cards advertisement

A. Pearson Company of Minneapolis advertised prices with simple graphics.

companies covered towns whose population and tourism appeal were too low to attract the big publishers like Curt Teich and E. C. Kropp.

The A. Pearson Company is typical of the real-photo postcard companies that produced black-and-white real-photo postcards from the 1920s through the 1950s. Owner Adolf Pearson employed salesmen-photographers to ride trains and drive cars to small towns in Minnesota, the

Dakotas, Iowa, and Wisconsin. Their job was to drum up sales with local vendors like drugstores, photograph the scenes that were requested, and deliver the black-and-white real-photo postcards to the buyer posthaste. Typically, the main street, courthouse, schools, and churches were photographed every ten to twenty years to keep the views current. The Minneapolis headquarters housed a production photo lab that could make the 5-by-7 negatives into 3½-by-5½ postcards in a few days.

About the time that chrome cards became the standard, fewer and fewer views of each town were included in a publisher's line, and finally, by the 1970s, fewer and fewer towns. Only big cities and tourist-centered communities commissioned cards, usually of a local landmark, a giant sculpture at the edge of town, or the nearest park, lake, or river. The final disappearance of main street came as postcard photographers turned to the surrounding landscape and photographed, for example, a canoe on a lake to represent "Ely." As we look at postcards made of our favorite hometown over the years, its distinctive features gradually disappear before our eyes. Commerce dictates what we can see. No wonder there is so much pleasure in discovering our town on a card made a hundred years ago.

Co-Mo salesman with car

He knows his business: a Co-Mo postcard salesman on the road in the early 1930s, his work advertised by this real-photo card.

Ely, Minnesota

Ely, Minnesota

This Cartwheel Company card uses a photograph by Jay Steinke to suggest that the bustling town of Ely, located near the Boundary Waters Canoe Area Wilderness, is a lovely lake in the mist.

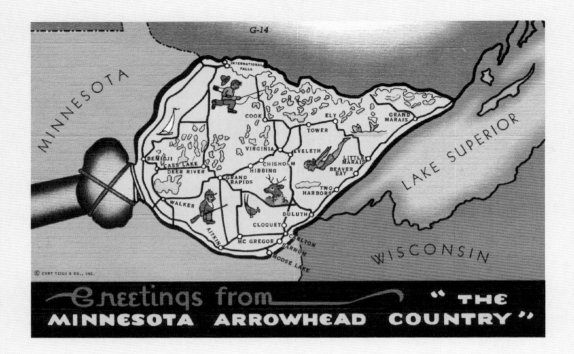

Greetings

The familiar "greetings from" cards began as German *Grüss Aus* cards at the dawn of postcard history. *Grüss* means "greetings," and for many years both words have been used as the opening to a tourist's postcard message.

Greetings from "The Minnesota Arrowhead Country"

This Curt Teich linen card from 1940 advertises the northeastern Minnesota "Arrowhead" region, named in 1925 by a man from Pittsburgh. Area businessmen created a regional commerce association in 1924 and then ran a contest to give their new organization a name, offering a prize of five hundred dollars. "Arrowhead" was chosen because it reflects the shape of the region and its Native American heritage.

Souvenir Greeting from Kerkhoven, Minn.

Kerkhoven's hometown photographer, Charles L. Merryman, composed eight of his own views, including three panoramas, into this busy and colorful souvenir, further ornamented with flowers and a leaf border. The sender, "M H H," used the card in September 1911 to write, "Dear You, Isn't this fine weather for the fair? I can just see you now out in the rain ringing wet."

Greetings from Faribault, Minnesota

When this linen card was produced by E. C. Kropp in about 1930, the southern Minnesota town of Faribault was proud of its schools and its local peony farm. Prominently displayed in the letters on this card are the high school, a private academy called Shattuck, and the state school for the blind and deaf, along with the library, viaduct, and courthouse. Known as "the Peony Capital of the World," Faribault was home to the Brand Peony Farm, a nursery established in 1868 that promoted a peony festival from 1927 to 1929.

Greetings from St. Paul

This beautiful art nouveau card advertising St. Paul, made by a Chicago publisher, employs a rare design composed of tiny photographs and drawings of women and babies, most likely lifted from other cards by the same publisher. The white space gives the sender a place to write a message, the back being reserved for address and postmark only.

Bird's-eye View Waconia — Looking West.

Pub. for W. J. Scharmer

Bird's-eye View Waconia – Looking West

"Came out here last night to spend Sunday," reported the sender of this card made by the St. Paul Souvenir Company. The 1910 view from Waconia's public school roof looks toward the peninsula in Lake Waconia. Just a few miles west of Lake Minnetonka, the lake was advertised as a "fisherman's mecca," accessible by railroad and featuring an island with a hotel and a billiard hall.

Biwabik, Minn.

Hunkered down for the winter on the eastern edge of the Mesabi Iron Range, Biwabik was photographed from aloft around 1910. The town's name means "iron" in Ojibwe, the language of the Native Americans who lived in the area. In 1891, Leonidas Merritt found high-grade iron ore near here, launching an industry that defined the region for many years. By the time this view was made, Biwabik housed three thousand residents, including workers from Scandinavia, Italy, and Austria-Hungary, who tolerated the subzero temperatures to make a living in the mines.

From the Bird's Eye

The term "bird's-eye view" was used by artists and lithographers long before it was enthusiastically adopted by the postcard industry. In the nineteenth century, artists were commissioned to portray whole towns in an imaginary overview such as a bird might have. Early bird's-eye postcard photographs were made from the tops of tall buildings, grain elevators, and water towers. Later, airplanes took the photographer to new heights, and aerial views showed a bigger piece of earth in less detail.

BIWABIK. MINN.

4th of July Parade, Sauk Center Minn. and Sauk Centre, MN

These two views of Sauk Centre, the model for the town of Gopher Prairie in Sinclair Lewis's novel Main Street, *illustrate changing visual values among postcard makers. In 1915, postcard buyers liked to see their towns busy and in some detail, as shown in the real-photo view by photographers Johnson and Olson of Alexandria. By 1994, the publisher NMN knew that an abstract overview with some graphic touches would attract customers accustomed to visual shorthand and less interested in street scene particulars.*

Mississippi River, St. Cloud, Minn.

Mississippi River
St. Cloud, Minn.

Around 1910, the photographer of this Bloom Brothers view captured two of St. Cloud's outstanding features: the river and the residences. The Mississippi River is crossed by a Great Northern Railroad bridge in the foreground and the St. Germain Street bridge in the background. In 1907, the St. Cloud Journal Press unobjectively declared this central Minnesota town one of the "handsomest" residence cities in the United States.

Souvenir of Hector Minn., Market Festival Oct. 15–16–1907.

A composite view of Hector's main street inside a cob of corn was a special souvenir of the third annual market festival. Prizes were awarded for local crops—including corn, of course—and the festivities included the entertaining "Comedy Hay Wagon Rube act" and "Sensational Brick Wall act." Katherine, who sent this card to Ella in Bird Island, reported, "We have a beautiful day for the carnival. We teachers are going to play basketball against the girls team this p.m."

Main Street, Lamberton, Minn.

Snow pictured on postcards usually illustrates record accumulations. Here Lamberton's normal winter look is featured on a hand-tinted card made in France in 1910, when 652 inhabitants called this their main street. Postcards were part of a far-reaching distribution system that transported this scene from Lamberton to France and back to southwestern Minnesota. French, German, and British printers surpassed the United States in quality and value at this early date.

Main Streets

Main streets were the staple of the postcard industry from 1900 to 1950. Almost every small town in Minnesota has at least one main street card to visually represent it. These cards document towns that most other photographers forgot and thus provide the best visual resource for studying rural Minnesota. But as the popularity of real-photo town cards waned in the 1950s, when generic landscape and recreation scenes took over, main street cards became the exception rather than the rule.

Main Street, LAMBERTON, MINN.

Birch Ave., Maple Lake, Minn.

A bustling downtown symbolizes prosperity. This main street in central Minnesota outstrips many "busy day" cards with sixty people and seventeen horse-drawn vehicles posing for the camera. Maple Lake's postmaster and newspaper publisher, Albert W. Nary, sponsored this card, published by the St. Paul Souvenir Company in 1908.

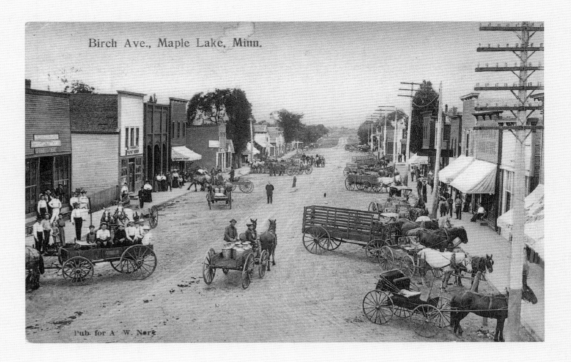

Bemidji, Minn.

Located on Lake Bemidji, this northern Minnesota town was ten years old and undergoing rapid growth when this 1915 real-photo postcard was distributed by Reynolds and Winter, land developers prominently advertised in the view captured by local photographer Niels Hakkerup. By 1920, there were fourteen businesses selling and developing land in this town of 7,086 people.

Street Scene, Backus, Minn.

Street scene, Backus, Minn.

Judging from this view—a hand-tinted postcard printed in Germany for Backus's postmaster, F. W. Zaffke—the town's main street is a rail line. In fact, this is not far from the truth, as the tracks for the Minnesota and International Railroad provided a major artery for the north-central Minnesota town, located in the heart of timber country and named for lumberman Edward W. Backus.

Main Street, International Falls

In 1953, residents of International Falls, a town perched on the Canadian border, could see Scared Stiff, starring Dean Martin and Jerry Lewis, at the Border movie theater. The Hamilton Photo Company of Ames, Iowa, made this warm weather view, a marked contrast to the customary wintertime look of the town known as the "Ice Box of the Nation."

Post Office, New Ulm, Minn.

Proud of their heritage, the citizens of New Ulm erected a German Renaissance–style post office in 1910. This homage to Germanity is made of alternating layers of brick and terra cotta with a roof of gray slate. The southwestern Minnesota town it serves is full of reminders of the Germans who settled there in 1854, and, of course, this Co-Mo Company card was printed in Germany, around the time the post office opened.

Carnegie Library, Browns Valley, Minn.

Steel baron Andrew Carnegie financed libraries like this one all over the United States, donating funds to small communities for "free public library services and architecturally sophisticated public library buildings." In 1913, the citizens of Browns Valley in western Minnesota received $5,500 from the Carnegie foundation to build their library. The neatly patterned brick façades on the classical revival building were completed in 1916, and it was used as a library until 1997.

POST OFFICE, NEW ULM, MINN.

CARNEGIE LIBRARY
BROWNS VALLEY, MINN.

Building Blocks

Everytown, U.S.A., has buildings that function in standard ways—library, post office, school, church, courthouse—and everyone understands that these buildings are essential to a town's daily operations. During the golden age of postcards and up until World War II, these buildings were regularly depicted on postcards, and buyers seemed content to send them as markers of a place. But after World War II, postcard images of a town's infrastructure declined in popularity, and tourist attractions and general views became the first choice for representing hometowns.

Public School, Mentor, Minn.

Public School, Mentor, Minn.

Hundreds of country schools dotted the Minnesota landscape when this postcard was published for Christine A. Messelt, Mentor's local postmistress and general store owner. According to the sign on the front, this aptly named school was built in 1900. Following a standard plan for schoolhouses, it has an access ladder to the bell tower and chimney. The 1914 message on the back of this postcard reads, "Arrived here all O.K. . . . Tell Papa I need more than $15."

Goodhue Co. Court House, Red Wing, Minn.

Goodhue Co. Court House, Red Wing, Minn.

Built in 1859, this Victorian courthouse served the citizens of Red Wing until 1931, when it was replaced by an art deco cube. The small building at the back was the town jail, added in 1887. Red Wing photographer Edward Lidberg made this card around 1910, arranging the scene to include a horse and buggy trotting down Fifth Street.

Bethlehem Kirke, St. Paul, Minn.

In 1890, a German Presbyterian congregation hired Cass Gilbert, architect of the state capitol, to design their church, which they occupied until 1916. This A. C. Bosselman card shows off architecture meant to resemble a medieval Swiss mountain parish church. The German company that printed the card used the German word for church, kirke, in the caption, perhaps at the congregation's request.

Roosevelt High School, Virginia, Minn. 1500 Children.

Virginia was a booming iron-mining town when this card, sponsored by local photographer Otto Moilan, was published by the St. Paul Souvenir Company in 1909. According to the Virginia Enterprise historical souvenir of the same year, the town's leaders believed the children of its many immigrant miners should be well educated toward "the American spirit and the American way of doing things." Those sentiments of civic pride probably explain why so many of Roosevelt High School's students are pictured, while most school postcards focus on the building alone.

Bethlehem Kirke, ST. PAUL, Minn.   10298

Roosevelt High School, Virginia, Minn. 1500 Children.

Grain Elevators, Adrian, Minn.

Grain Elevators, Adrian, Minn.

Elevator Row, Minnesota Lake, Minn.

Elevator Row, Minnesota Lake, Minn.

Prairie Cathedrals

Grain elevators are the skyscrapers of the countryside, built along railroad lines that carried wheat, oats, barley, rye, and flax from local farms to the world. Instead of tall office buildings symbolizing wealth and progress, rural Minnesota has elevators, conducting the business of agriculture by storing harvested grain.

Looking at these prairie giants, one might wonder what goes on inside and why they are so tall. The answer is that elevators are huge grain storage bins that are filled from the top, allowing gravity to do much of the work. When a farmer pulls up to the elevator and dumps his harvested grain into a bin, a series of carriers on a conveyor belt lifts the grain to the top. One of the elevator workers selects a bin for the grain and it falls, via chute, into

the right storage tube. Later, a train comes along to receive the grain from another chute that drops it into a rail car. From there it starts its journey to the world.

Three of these four early postcards show towns in southern Minnesota on the Iowa border: Adrian, Minnesota Lake, and Emmons. Herman, in far western Minnesota, lies near the Dakota border. All are on railroad lines owned by different companies at the time these cards were made, around 1910. The modern chrome view of Red Wing includes an elevator complex that processes and stores grain on a larger scale than the others. Several railroad lines run past the Red Wing elevators on their way east to Chicago.

Grain Elevators, Herman, Minn.

Emmons railroad depot and grain elevator

Bird's-eye view of Red Wing and its towering elevators

Alworth Building, Duluth, Minn.

In September 1922, a visitor from Minneapolis wrote on this Curt Teich card, "Am home now. This is one of the big office buildings of Duluth. Not much when compared to the Railway Exchange?" At the time, the Alworth Building was the sixteen-story wonder of Duluth, built of reinforced concrete and steel in a record nine months in 1910. The local press described it as "one that dwarfs the tower of Babel to a mere cottage in comparison."

The Big City

City postcards usually feature different scenes than small town cards do. Typically, city cards display a prominent commercial building or a skyline view, whereas town cards may feature a main street, a public building, or a bird's-eye view. When it comes to the production of postcards, a noticeable difference between small and large towns is that the majority of small-town views are real-photo cards and the majority of city views are color-printed cards. This distinction has to do with the size of the market. Real-photo cards can be printed in small quantities, say one hundred at a time for commercial sales, whereas color-printed cards are usually ordered by the thousands.

Glass Block, Minneapolis

With its many windows, Donaldson's Glass Block on Nicollet and Sixth was the perfect building to be represented in this "hold to the light" postcard made around 1905. With the aid of a light source, the viewer sees the windows illuminated from behind. This magnificent Minneapolis department store, built in 1888, was designed to be filled with light in contrast to dark general stores that folks might have back in their hometowns. During the 1940s the lovely exterior was covered over, and the lights went out in 1982 when the building was demolished.

"Minneapolis–St. Paul Postcard Fantasy"

◀ *In honor of National Postcard Week, in May 1992 the Twin City Postcard Club issued this view of St. Paul joined to Minneapolis. Ann-Marie Rose created the impossible scene from thirteen separate images, including the Hubert H. Humphrey Metrodome on the left and the St. Paul Ice Palace on the right. At the time, computer imaging was just beginning to enter the postcard scene.*

Sky Line and Union Depot Yards, St. Paul, Minn.

This perspective from Dayton's Bluff, published by the H. A. Olson Specialty Company, showcases the major role railroads played in 1930s St. Paul. The Great Northern and Northern Pacific Railroads used these yards to bring people and products to the town of 271,606.

COURT HOUSE, ST. PAUL, MINNESOTA—9 INDIAN GOD OF PEACE

Court House, St. Paul, Minnesota (with Indian God of Peace)

A landmark on the St. Paul skyline since 1932, the twenty-story courthouse has as its focal point an impressive thirty-six-foot onyx sculpture of an Indian standing in a dark blue marble hall with a mirrored ceiling. The Vision of Peace was created by Swedish sculptor Carl Milles. This linen postcard by E. C. Kropp reflects the moderne styling of the building designed by Holabird and Root of Chicago and Ellerby and Company of St. Paul.

FOSHAY TOWER, MINNEAPOLIS, MINN.

2518-29

Foshay Tower, Minneapolis, Minn.

Just before the Great Depression began in 1929, millionaire real estate developer Wilbur B. Foshay financed this art deco variation of the Washington Monument. The Foshay Tower's structure of steel and reinforced concrete was faced with Indiana limestone, and only the best materials, such as African mahogany and Italian marble, were used inside. The John Philip Sousa Band marked the grand opening with a new piece: the "Foshay Tower–Washington Memorial March," commissioned by Foshay for the occasion. But this lavish expenditure proved overly optimistic in the face of the stock market crash: Foshay lost the building to creditors a year later. Curt Teich printed this white-border card in 1929.

40

IDS Center

IDS Center

The IDS Center, constructed for Investors Diversified Services, replaced the Foshay Tower as the tallest building in Minneapolis in 1972. Architects Philip Johnson, John Burgee, and Ed Baker designed the building so that each of fifty-seven floors has thirty-two corner offices. Its reflective surface is made of 42,614 panes of glass, enough for one pair of sunglasses for each resident of Minnesota, Wisconsin, and the two Dakotas. Nathaniel Lieberman took the photo for this chrome postcard soon after the building was completed.

The Clinic, Rochester, Minn.

Patients have been seeking help in this fifteen-story building since it opened in 1928 as one of the first group medical practices in the United States, housing 386 doctors and dentists, 288 examining rooms, and 21 laboratories. The eclectic revival style includes Moorish details in its trim, an elaborately decorated interior, and a carillon bell tower commemorating World War I veterans. E. C. Kropp published this card for the Rochester News Agency in 1940.

THE CLINIC,
ROCHESTER, MINN.—42

Noteworthy Events

Photographers and postcard publishers saw dollar signs when they observed natural disasters and local celebrations. Small-town photographers rushed to the scenes of weather events and parades to capture on film what the local newspaper could not include on its pages. While the historical sleuth can find detailed descriptions of these events reported in the newspapers of the time, photographs were too expensive to print alongside the text. From about 1900 to 1920, many real-photo postcards were published to spread and enhance local news. Color postcards were made to commemorate bigger events that would sell to a broader audience.

Almost every Minnesota town has a special celebration, some with great names like Boxelder Bug Days in Minneota or the Tree Frog Music Festival in Faribault. Other towns throw parties on holidays like the Fourth of July or when the carnival comes to town. Most of these fun fests occur in summer, when every Minnesotan feels like celebrating. But once in a while the wild and crazy among us venture out in cold weather to attend a gathering like the Walker Eelpout Festival or the St. Paul Winter Carnival.

Fergus Falls cyclone

More than thirty different postcards were published after a cyclone hit Fergus Falls, Minnesota, on June 22, 1919. The storm came on a Sunday afternoon and lasted only twenty minutes but left fifty-three dead and 118 homes destroyed. Just across the Red River from this view, the Grand Hotel "went down like an eggshell" according to the Fergus Falls Daily Journal. Ironically, the collapse killed its owner, who had just bought the property and arrived in town ten minutes before the cyclone struck.

ROTARY STEAM SNOW SHOVEL AT WORK · NEW ULM MINN ·
Feb 27-09

Fourth of July float, Kerkhoven

Independence Day inspires parades, costumes, and floats throughout Minnesota. In this real-photo card from Kerkhoven on July 4, 1913, local photographer Charles L. Merryman captured lady liberty and an angel, each in their own spiffed-up parade cars. Lady Liberty is Blanch Westerdahl. The angel, fifteen-year-old Genevieve Negaard, grew up to become a teacher and a Republican Party fundraiser, eventually having tea with Mary Pickford and meeting the King and Queen of Norway.

Rotary Steam Snow Shovel at Work, New Ulm, Minn.

◀ *Three big blizzards blew through New Ulm in January and February 1909. After the third one hit on February 27, huge walls of snow blocked train travel in southern Minnesota. "New Ulm Isolated by Big Blizzard" was the newspaper headline, underscoring that the railroad was the area's lifeline. The railroad itself came to the rescue with huge snow-throwing, plow-fronted engines that cleared the tracks, with spectacular effects.*

Mamouth Hail Stone Found by M. C. O'Mahony, Pipestone, Minn.

Imagine bringing a hailstone into a photographer's studio to pose for a portrait. Mr. O'Mahony was front-page news in the September 19, 1911, Pipestone County Star, having picked up the five pounder the morning after the storm dropped it through a skylight in the land office. "There were persons who couldn't believe all of this story," commented the reporter, who also noted that hundreds of chickens were killed or maimed by "hailstones as large as hens eggs."

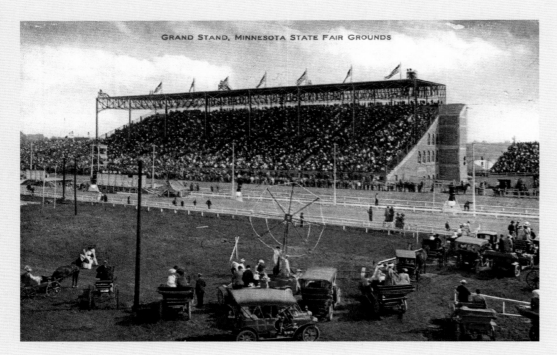

GRAND STAND, MINNESOTA STATE FAIR GROUNDS

Grand Stand, Minnesota State Fair Grounds

The Minnesota State Fair, held at the end of August in St. Paul, is one of the largest in the country. This V. O. Hammon card from about 1910 shows the grandstand that was constructed in 1909, the fiftieth year of the fair. The weblike radio antenna set up in the center of this scene may be for broadcasting a horse race, perhaps one against the famous, never-beaten Dan Patch.

Scene at Minnesota State Fair Grounds

The lamp at the front of this V. O. Hammon card indicates the electrification of the Minnesota state fairgrounds in 1899, encouraging hordes of fairgoers to continue strolling past the exhibits and vendors' tents late into the evening. The grandstand visible on the horizon was replaced in 1909.

SCENE AT MINNESOTA STATE FAIR GROUNDS

Colorful Floats in Aquatennial Parade, Minneapolis, Minn.

Minneapolis created a major summer festival—the Aquatennial—in 1942 to accentuate its sobriquet, the City of Lakes. Like St. Paul's winter festival, the centerpiece is a parade. In this linen Curt Teich postcard from 1949, floats proceed down Nicollet Avenue, Minneapolis's main street at the time.

Carnival in Laurel Street, Brainerd, Minn.

While today Brainerd townsfolk find sidewalk sales and craft festivals on Main Street, in 1910 they found a carnival there. This hand-tinted card, published by A. M. Simon of New York, shows how a business street was transformed into a festive corridor.

Ice Palace, St. Paul, Minn.

7A-H2541

Ice Palace, St. Paul, Minn.

Cold can be fun! The St. Paul Winter Carnival began in 1886 when the capital city decided it needed an attraction to counteract its reputation for numbing cold. What better way than with lively parades, toboggan slides, and snowshoe treks? This linen Curt Teich card shows the 1937 ice palace, built in front of the state capitol building and designed by African American architect Cap Wigington.

International Eelpout Festival

Held every year in the dead of winter, the International Eelpout Festival has attracted as many as ten thousand people to stand on frozen Leech Lake in Walker, Minnesota, and catch a slimy fish that looks like a cross between a catfish and an eel. A member of the cod family, the eelpout spawns in winter and is as foolhardy as the people who fish for it. This 1994 card by Peter Hawkins displays one amazing catch.

Three Grades of Prisoners, Minnesota State Prison

A series of cards published in 1909 by W. C. Heilbron reflected the strong public interest in Stillwater's prison, an important local landmark that housed notorious prisoners like Cole Younger. A note on the back of this card indicates that each grade of prisoner gains more privileges, the greatest number upon reaching "first grade."

Women Inmates in Prison Yard, Minnesota State Prison

From 1853 to 1912, the Minnesota State Prison in Stillwater housed all state offenders, including ten women in 1909, the date of this postcard. The women likely faced away from John Runk's camera for privacy, or because they were about to receive instructions from the matron at left.

Unique Features

Each Minnesota town seeks a distinctive feature, whether one that provides jobs and attracts commerce or one that draws tourists. In the nineteenth and early twentieth centuries, politicians competed to have an institution like a prison or hospital built in their town, just as later they competed for industry to settle there. Planners and leaders were also busy developing parks and other amenities to bring more residents and attract tourists.

Spiral Bridge, Hastings, Minn.

Perhaps no other bridge in Minnesota is as beloved and remembered as the Hastings spiral bridge, built in 1895 and demolished in 1951. Designed to provide clearance for the smokestacks of steamboats navigating the Mississippi River, it deposited car traffic in the center of downtown Hastings. There were many postcards published of this bridge, this one made in the 1920s by the Co-Mo Company.

Main Building, State Hospital for the Insane, St. Peter, Minn.

This bucolic scene may reflect the mood desired by administrators of this hospital for the mentally ill, established in 1866 in the small southern Minnesota town of St. Peter. By 1910, when this card was published by V. O. Hammon, the hospital housed 1,169 patients, 28 percent of the town's population.

Indian Mounds, St. Paul, Minn.

In this 1906 V. O. Hammon postcard, a genteel family enjoys an outing next to two-thousand-year-old Indian burial mounds located in St. Paul. Mounds Park was deemed "one of the chief points of interest to visitors in the city" in an 1897 report, one year after several mounds had been removed. The park was expanded in 1900 and further landscaped between 1904 and 1907.

Japanese Garden, Como Park. St. Paul, Minn.

A nook on Cozy Lake in St. Paul's Como Park was exotically outfitted when Dr. R. Schiffman donated his collection of Japanese trees and shrubs, purchased at the 1904 St. Louis World's Fair. The deep greens of the shrubbery are accented on this Polychrome card made in Germany and published by the Minnesota News Company of St. Paul.

Japanese Garden, Como Park. St. Paul, Minn.

Minneapolis, Minn., Minnehaha Falls

Over 250 postcards have been published of Minnehaha Falls, made famous by Henry Wadsworth Longfellow in The Song of Hiawatha. *His poem, inspired by a Minnesotan's daguerreotype, made the south Minneapolis site a must-see for tourists. It soon became a favorite picnic and strolling venue, where visitors could buy a postcard like this one by Hugh Leighton of Portland, Maine, made in 1910.*

Minneapolis, Minn., Minnehaha Falls.

View from Top of Famous Incline Railway, Duluth, Minn.

After 1891, visitors to Duluth could descend one-half mile from the Duluth Heights trolley line to the main street via incline railway. The railway made the upper reaches of the town, overlooking Lake Superior and Minnesota Point, accessible and desirable—a boon to real estate developers. This linen card from 1937 was published by Curt Teich two years before the railway was closed.

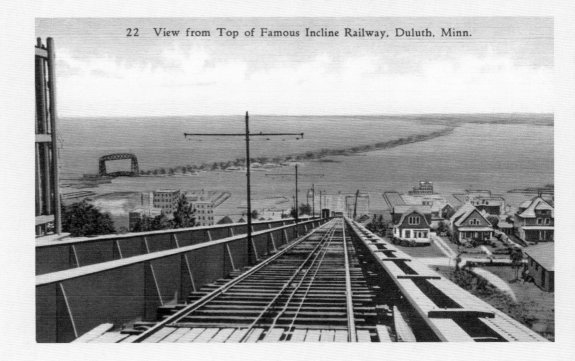

22 View from Top of Famous Incline Railway, Duluth, Minn.

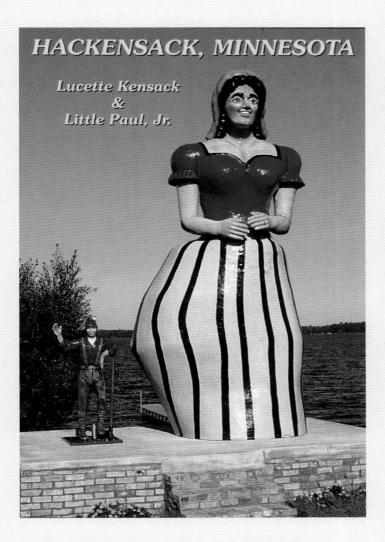

HACKENSACK, MINNESOTA

Lucette Kensack
&
Little Paul, Jr.

Hackensack, Minnesota, Lucette Kensack & Little Paul, Jr.

Did Paul Bunyan need a girlfriend? Promoters for Hackensack sought a gimmick for their town, and in the 1950s they created Paul's sweetheart for tourists to stop and see on their way to Bemidji from Brainerd. They also invented a festival for her called Sweetheart Day. There is no record of when Paul and Lucette were married, but Paul Junior appeared on the scene in 1992, after which D. J. Nordgren of NMN made this postcard view.

Paul & Babe, Bemidji, MN

More than thirty-five Paul Bunyan statues have been erected by local communities around the United States. Minnesota's oldest has been standing with his sidekick, Babe, alongside Lake Bemidji since 1937. Created as a marketing symbol for the Weyerhaeuser Lumber Company, Paul became a tourist attraction after he was employed to draw visitors to the Bemidji Winter Carnival.

Larger than Life

City leaders are always inventing new ways to promote their towns. In 1937, Bemidji planners came up with the idea for a giant statue of Paul Bunyan, the legendary lumberjack, to accompany their local celebration. It was so successful in bringing attention to

the town that others soon followed suit. By the 1970s, oversize statues of everything imaginable had surfaced all over the state. Postcard makers focused on these novelties, and now dozens of towns are represented by local titans, behemoths, and record-setting feats. These images have replaced views of main street and the county courthouse as postcard symbols of Minnesota's rural towns. In fact, according to the website roadsideamerica.com, Minnesota and North Dakota boast the densest population of giant animals anywhere on earth.

The Worlds Biggest Tiger Muskie, Nevis, Minn.

Of the twenty-four super-sized fish statues in Minnesota, the Nevis Tiger Muskie is among the oldest. Warren Ballard, taxidermist, gas station owner, and muskie grower, fashioned this whopper out of concrete on a wood frame in 1949. The local chamber of commerce was considering adopting a log cabin as the town symbol until Mr. Ballard convinced them a muskie was a better mascot for a town located in the lakes area of northwestern Minnesota.

Snowman, North St. Paul, Minn.

North St. Paulites are justly proud of their year-round snowman, who stands smiling at the edge of a highway and bike trail between St. Paul and Stillwater. His 20-ton, 44-foot body was built of steel, rebar, and stucco in 1972–74 by local businessmen, inspired by a successful showing of a giant snowy snowman at the town's winter festival. This mid-seventies chrome card was issued in his honor.

Father of Waters, Court House Rotunda, Minneapolis, Minn.

Lounging in a five-story court, the fourteen-thousand-pound Father of Waters gazes upon visitors to Minneapolis's city hall. Sculptor Larkin Mead modeled the artwork after the Greek Father Nile sculpture, using Italian Carrara marble to equip him with an Indian blanket, cornstalk, fish net, alligator, and terrapin, symbolizing the regions touched by the Mississippi River after it leaves Minneapolis. A. C. Bosselman published the card shortly after the building opened in 1905.

Jolly Green Giant

Weighing in at eight thousand pounds, the Jolly Green Giant was born as a trademark of the Minnesota Valley Canning Company of Le Sueur, Minnesota, and is now the commercial property of General Mills. He was created in 1925 to promote the valley's big peas, hence his color and size. The fifty-five-foot roadside statue appeared at the side of Interstate 90 in 1978, the year the superhighway was completed near Blue Earth in southern Minnesota.

Francis A. Johnson and his ball of twine

For twenty-nine years, Francis A. Johnson added to a ball of twine in his front yard in Darwin, Minnesota, eventually achieving the distinction of owning the world's largest. Now enshrined in a main street gazebo, it weighs 17,400 pounds and is twelve feet wide and eleven feet high. Johnson, who died a bachelor in 1989, was the son of U.S. senator Magnus Johnson of Minnesota. This appropriately super-sized 6-by-9-inch chrome postcard was printed by Bankers Advertising Company of Iowa City, Iowa.

Big Ole   *Alexandria, Minnesota*

Big Ole, Alexandria, Minnesota

Minnesota's Scandinavians celebrated their Viking heritage by creating the giant "Big Ole" for the 1964–65 New York World's Fair. This proud fellow is twenty-eight feet tall and weighs four tons. At the fair he stood near the Kensington rune stone, a controversial piece of archaeology that reputedly contains an inscription by Vikings who visited the area in 1362, thus making Alexandria the "Birthplace of America."

"World's Largest Lefsa"

"World's Largest Lefsa"

Starbuck, a west-central Minnesota community settled by Norwegians, celebrated its centennial in 1983 by creating a giant lefse. Made from thirty pounds of potatoes, thirty-five pounds of flour, one pound of sugar, and four pounds of shortening, the lefse measured nine feet and eight inches across and weighed seventy pounds. NMN postcard company captured this historic event, which is also recorded in the Schibstad Book of Records in Norway. A festival called Lefse Days was subsequently invented to commemorate this great achievement.

CHAPTER TWO

Our Business

Dear _____:

While at the Minnesota State Fair I plan to visit the large factory illustrated on the other side. They tell me that here, under one roof are manufactured a larger variety of foods than are manufactured in any other similiar [sic] organization in the United States. I am anxious to see it because they say you can see raw food products from every corner of the globe magically transpire before your eyes into appetizing goodies in packaging so familiar at our grocers. Am having a wonderful time.

Best regards, _____

Preprinted message on a Griggs Cooper postcard

dvertising postcards have a long history, from nineteenth-century salesmen's stock to today's junk mailings. Quick to see the economy of transmitting business messages on a one-cent card, merchants were among the first senders of postcards in Minnesota. Announcements of sales, prices, and impending vendor visits fill the message space on many early cards. Such abbreviated business communication was possible as early as 1873, when the U.S. Post Office issued government postcards along with a set of regulations on their use. Business correspondence was encouraged: "They may therefore be used for order, invitation, notices, receipts, acknowledgments, price lists, and other requirements of business and society life." Cards in this early period included few illustrations. In order to travel for one cent, the card had to be printed by the U.S. government. The preprinted side included a stamp mark and lines for the address, and the plain back side could carry the advertiser's message, which was often verbal rather than pictorial. For this reason, most early business postcards are rather plain.

The Private Mailing Card Act of 1898 permitted printers other than the U.S. government to make cards, and as a result the genre of pictorial business postcards blos-

56

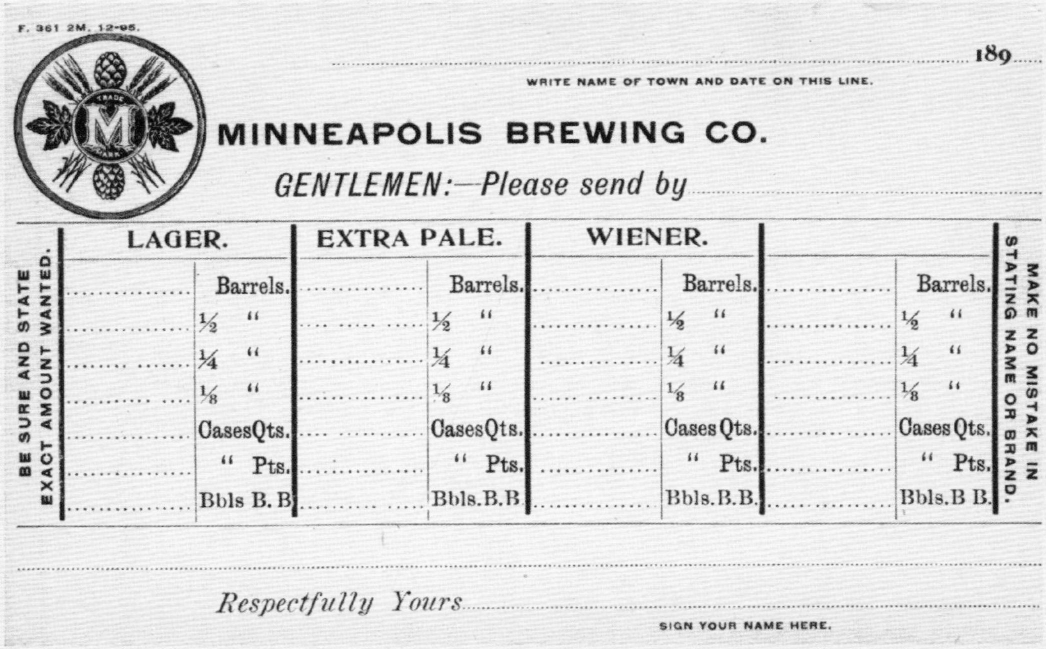

F. 361 2M. 12-95.

189

WRITE NAME OF TOWN AND DATE ON THIS LINE.

MINNEAPOLIS BREWING CO.

GENTLEMEN:—Please send by

BE SURE AND STATE EXACT AMOUNT WANTED.

LAGER.		EXTRA PALE.		WIENER.			
	Barrels.		Barrels.		Barrels.		Barrels.
	½ "		½ "		½ "		½ "
	¼ "		¼ "		¼ "		¼ "
	⅛ "		⅛ "		⅛ "		⅛ "
	Cases Qts.		Cases Qts.		Cases Qts.		Cases Qts.
	" Pts.		" Pts.		" Pts.		" Pts.
	Bbls. B.B		Bbls. B.B		Bbls. B.B.		Bbls. B.B.

MAKE NO MISTAKE IN STATING NAME OR BRAND.

Respectfully Yours

SIGN YOUR NAME HERE.

Minneapolis Brewing Company

This 1890s order card for the Minneapolis Brewing Company, maker of Gilt Edge Beer and Golden Grain Belt Beer, allowed patrons to keep their bars stocked by simply filling out and returning a postcard.

somed. Among the many companies to take advantage of this new color advertising medium was Brown & Bigelow of St. Paul. From the golden age of postcards through the 1930s, it printed calendar postcards for companies all over the United States and Canada. Each one carried a color illustration by a popular artist and included a prepunched hole so that recipients could hang the appealing view on their wall. In the early years the postcards featured beautiful women and children or scenes of home and fireside.

The cards were overprinted to order, some with calendars and some with advertising copy. Or the client could choose a business message such as "a salesman will call," with a line for the date, or the cheery greeting, "your insurance premium is due." Beyond reminders, the empty space on the back could announce sales, facilitate hotel reservations, solicit votes, and provide a convenient way to order goods. Of course, the most common use of business postcards was to directly advertise by illustration and preprinted message. Some card backs were completely filled with the advertisement, leaving no room for recipients to

I expect to call upon you on or about_____
with the Brown & Bigelow calendar line for 1909.
    This line cost just a little short of twice as much
as its famous predecessor for 1908.
    It will pay you to see it.

                Yours truly,

BROWN & BIGELOW
The House of Quality
ST. PAUL, U. S. A.

Brown & Bigelow, The House of Quality, St. Paul, U.S.A.

A 1908 Brown & Bigelow postcard announced the imminent arrival of a calendar salesman.

use the card themselves. Many were discarded, but yesterday's junk mail becomes today's collectible, saved in scrapbooks and postcard collections and, in many cases, depicting businesses that otherwise would not have been recorded.

The postcard is alive and well as a tool of commerce. In fact, a new kind of advertising postcard emerged in the 1990s. Called a "rack card," this giveaway is displayed in restaurants and bars, at music stores, and on college campuses. Rack cards advertise everything from food and liquor to merchandise and entertainment and are published by companies with names like GoCARD and m@x RACKS. Customers are free to take as many as they want for posting and collecting. Rack cards have found their place in postcard history: today's postcard dealers offer them for sale at shows and write about them in *Postcard Collector* magazine.

Custom Cards for the Advertising Customer

Beginning with Brown & Bigelow, Minnesota postcard publishers recognized a market for "custom" printed cards—promotional cards ordered by a business and distributed by its customers, not by the publisher. When the appetite for view cards diminished, many national publishers like Curt Teich increased production by offering their services to independent busi-

R. Steinman & Co. ad card

◀ *R. Steinman, a St. Paul postcard publisher, took advantage of a practical method to solicit requests: send a postcard photograph to the local drugstore with a convenient order form on its reverse side.*

NFL Originals Exclusively at

◎

KELLIE RAE THEISS GALLERY PRESENTS KELLY CONNOLE

EVENING RECEPTION: FRIDAY, OCTOBER 26, 2001

Kellie Rai Theiss Gallery Presents Kelly Connole

Minneapolis's Kellie Rai Theiss Gallery used a postcard image of the "Jackalope's Feeble Attempt at Rebellion" to announce a show of Kelly Connole's artwork, advertising her "three dimensional dialog" and her ability to "write novels in clay."

NFL Originals Exclusively at Target

Minnesota's Target Corporation used this GoCARD to introduce a line of apparel.

59

nesses looking for an inexpensive, eye-catching advertising medium.

A big boost to this aspect of the postcard business came with the increased number of resorts established in Minnesota in the 1930s, '40s, and '50s. Like hotels, resorts provided the perfect venue for postcards, replete as they were with eager tourists who had plenty of idle time for writing. Companies like W. A. Fisher of Virginia, Minnesota, and L. L. Cook of Milwaukee, Wisconsin, printed as many resort cards as they did general view cards. That market has now faded, and contemporary companies like Cartwheel of St. Paul receive custom orders mainly from attractions like the Mall of America's Camp Snoopy, as well as casinos, historic sites, museums, and zoos.

Custom cards distributed by hotels and motels usually have preprinted captions describing amenities designed to appeal to the traveler of the time. These suggest an evolution in tourist demands and desires. For example, most cards published prior to World War II assure the guest that the lodging is fireproof at a time when hotel fires were common disasters. In the 1920s, a guest at the Curtis Hotel in Minneapolis would be thrilled to discover "pipe organ recitals at noon, [and] orchestra and dancing six to eight o'clock each evening." Forty years later, people staying at the Minneapolis Sheraton Ritz were lured by air-conditioning, a "garden" swimming pool, and "three great

restaurants catering to gourmet tastes." Bathroom facilities are frequently mentioned as well. Initially the number of bathrooms was the issue, as Duluth's Hotel Lenox advertised "200 rooms, 100 with bath" on its 1926 postcards. Subsequently, "private baths" and then "ceramic baths" were listed as special features. Motel postcards provide long lists of offerings including indoor pools, child care, convention facilities, gourmet dining, piano bars, and VIP suites. All are details that can be read as signs of the time.

A somewhat different brand of custom card is the artist's self-promotional card. Photographers, craftspeople, and art galleries mail millions of postcards to illustrate their best work and announce upcoming shows. This is the one branch of card publishing that is seldom handled by the major postcard printers and publishers. Instead, artists or galleries use a convenient local printer and distribute the cards themselves.

Postcards have been an integral element of advertising from the very beginning. Evidence of their continued success arrives every day in the mail—and some of these are the collectibles of the future.

Canoe Country Outfitters

A perfect business for Ely, surrounded as it is by lakes and wilderness, Canoe Country ▶ *Outfitters has served explorers of northern Minnesota since 1946. Owners Bill and Barbara Rom provide canoes, supplies, maps, and sometimes guides to hundreds of nature seekers each year. This 1950 chrome card features their Chevrolet station wagon, an elegant transport into the woods.*

Corner store

Although not identified on this card, the purpose of this business can be revealed by a magnifying glass. Four of the men wear conductor uniforms, indicating that this corner may be a streetcar rest stop, probably in or near the Twin Cities. The posters in the window and on the wall advertise events in Minneapolis and St. Paul as well as products of St. Paul's Crescent Creamery. The clarity of this 1910 real-photo card allows careful viewers to study the raising mechanism for the awnings, admire the necklace worn by the female employee on the left, and read the advertisements for at least ten different brands of cigars. The unnamed store is typical of early real-photo postcards, which seldom carried captions unless the sender chose to write one on the back.

The Look Outside and In

Some small businesses are documented only on postcards and in local directories, so postcards allow a glimpse into operations that otherwise might be unrecorded. For larger businesses, like the Minneapolis Brewing Company, postcards are an interesting adjunct to corporate history.

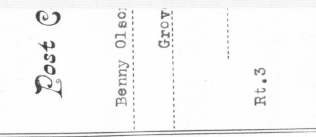

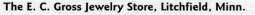

The E. C. Gross Jewelry Store, Litchfield, Minn.

Keeping Litchfield residents on time in more ways than one, Emil C. Gross sold jewelry and repaired watches from 1900 to 1929. In 1913, the year of this St. Paul Souvenir Company card, Mr. Gross held a removal sale, moving to another location and using postcards to advertise the resulting discounted prices in his store.

Plant of Zenith Furnace Co., at West Duluth, Minn.

Located in the "Zenith City," Duluth's huge pig iron blast furnace opened in 1904 and ran until the 1960s on 170 acres near Lake Superior. Though industrial sites rarely find their way onto today's postcards, this card suggests the beauty of the hardworking structures that served Minnesota's Iron Range.

PLANT OF ZENITH FURNACE CO. AT WEST DULUTH MINN

Stripping Overburden for Ore, Mesaba Iron Range, Minnesota

The huge steam shovel that overshadows the men in this view was a common sight on Minnesota's Iron Range in 1910, when this V. O. Hammon card was published. "Overburden," or topsoil covering ore-bearing ground, was removed via railcar, as was the ore collected from the open pit mines.

STRIPPING OVERBURDEN FOR ORE, MESABA IRON RANGE, MINNESOTA

The RANCH HOUSE
Food & Environment Dedicated To You
79th & Lyndale
So. on U. S. Highway 65
MINNEAPOLIS, MINNESOTA

Ranch House

The Ranch House, 79th and Lyndale, Minneapolis, Minnesota

When Midwest Specialties published this card in the 1950s, the Ranch House restaurant was located far outside Minneapolis, in the suburb of Bloomington, near the future path of Interstate 494. The owner, Harriet Long, ordered a multiview card so she could advertise her roadhouse inside and out.

Ortonville's Leading Business Firms

Ortonville State Bank · Palm's Jewelry Shop · "Schoen Pays the Freight" · Park Garage · First National Bank · Pioneer Co-Operative Department Store · Big Stone Lake Scene · Kollitz Mercantile Co. · Quality and Service · Schneider's · Columbian Hotel · Geier Lumber Co. · Home Yard · Nielson's Drug Store · Citizens National Bank · Vikre, PHOTOGRAPHER.

Ortonville's Leading Business Firms

October 14, 1915, was a banner day for the west-central Minnesota town of Ortonville, as visitors from sixteen counties and the Dakotas crowded the streets and the city park to participate in the Corn, Alfalfa and Grain Show given by the West Central Minnesota Development Association. This multiview postcard advertised the celebration, and its images, all made by local photographer Peter Vikre, also appeared in a special edition of the Ortonville Journal. Such cards provide a visual inventory of the era's typical small-town businesses—from banks to co-ops to hotels.

Nelson's Photo Studio, Little Falls, Minn.

With its light-catching windows, four thousand square feet of studio space, and an expansive second-floor living area, this state-of-the-art photo studio was the pride of its owner, Frank A. Nelson. From 1908 until 1936, Mr. Nelson photographed hundreds of Little Falls residents in his Broadway Street business, advertised in this 1920s Bloom Brothers card.

NELSON'S PHOTO STUDIO, LITTLE FALLS, MINN.   OUR PHOTOS SPEAK FOR THEMSELVES.

Tepeetoka Ice Cream Parlor at the Palace of Sweets, Winona, Minn.

The Palace of Sweets sold "confections"—candy, ice cream, and tropical fruits—in the Mississippi River town of Winona. Serving customers from the 1890s through the 1920s, the Kratz family devised many attractions, including an Indian motif at the back of the store on East Third Street, advertised as the Tepeetoka on this circa 1908 postcard.

TEPEETOKA ICE CREAM PARLOR
at the PALACE OF SWEETS, Winona, Minn.

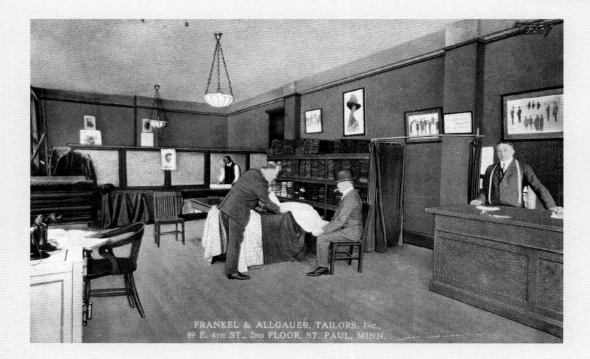

FRANKEL & ALLGAUER, TAILORS, INC.,
89 E. 4TH ST., 2ND FLOOR, ST. PAUL, MINN.

Frankel & Allgauer, Tailors, Inc., 89 E. 4th St., 2nd Floor, St. Paul, Minn.

In business from 1910 to 1922, Frankel & Allgauer suited both men and women. When Jules Frankel and George Allgauer hired the Curt Teich Company to make this postcard for them in 1917, St. Paul was home to 222 other tailors. The back of the card invites the recipient to "get tailorized," which included choosing fabrics and being measured for a new suit of clothes. Custom sewing was probably done in a back room.

R. M. CHAPMAN CO., MINNEAPOLIS. Grocers, Bakers, Confectioners.

R. M. Chapman Co., Minneapolis. Grocers, Bakers, Confectioners.

At the height of his business in 1915, Ralph M. Chapman commissioned this Curt Teich Octochrome postcard to promote his fancy new store in the Essex Building on Nicollet Avenue, Minneapolis's main shopping street. After twenty-one years in the grocery business at 732–734 Nicollet, Chapman set up shop in this brand-new building in 1912. But the move must have taxed his resources, for he left this location in 1916 and did not reopen his store elsewhere.

City Restaurant, Ashby, Minn.

Fishermen and hunters could gaze at stuffed versions of their prey in this western Minnesota restaurant. The 1958 real-photo card by the L. L. Cook firm shows great detail: cigars, cigarettes, pipe tobacco, and snuff line the shelves and countertops, depicting a time when the "no-smoking section" was unknown.

MAGIC AQUARIUM BAR AND LIQUOR STORE — MOORHEAD, MINN.

9A-H1920

Magic Aquarium Bar and Liquor Store, Moorhead, Minn.

"See the beautiful lights glowing from the ash trays placed on it. See the mixing spoons light up in your glasses as they are placed on the bar." According to the preprinted caption, the "magic bar" in Moorhead offered these visual delights plus an opportunity to view five hundred varieties of fish in its aquarium. Curt Teich made this card for the owners, Walter and Eva Seign, in the 1940s. Unfortunately for today's viewers, who may find themselves entranced by the scene and accompanying description, the Magic Aquarium Bar closed in 1970.

THIRD STREET CAFE
BEMIDJI, MINN.
*"The Most Popular Cafe
in the Northwest"*

Third Street Cafe, Bemidji, Minn.

According to the preprinted caption, the customer who sat down in the gleaming, modern Third Street Cafe was offered sizzling steaks, wall-eyed pike, fried chicken, barbecued ribs, and homemade pastries. Curt Teich produced this cheery linen card in 1950 for Hans L. Marcks, manager of the Bemidji restaurant that was open from 1917 to 1973 as "the place where friends meet."

Scene in
New
Bottling
House

Minneapolis
Brewing
Company

Scene in New Bottling House, Minneapolis Brewing Company

The makers of Grain Belt Beer were so successful in the early twentieth century that they built a new bottling house capable of processing 14,000 gallons of beer each day. The company employed over 250 people, a few of whom appear on this advertising card from about 1908. The preprinted message on the back evidences a time when the company promoted home consumption of beer as a healthy family activity.

POST CARD

CORRESPONDENCE HERE

NAME AND ADDRESS HERE

Have just been through the brewery where the popular Golden Grain Belt Beer is made. It's the cleanest place I ever saw. Had a Dutch Lunch and sampled the beer. It's fine and just the kind to have at home. Wish you were here.

Yours,

Fred

Miss Lora Noerenberg

Crystal Bay

Minnetonka

Hotel Duluth, Duluth, Minnesota

Looking more like a New York City hotel than a hostelry serving a town of one hundred thousand, the Hotel Duluth is chic and modern on this Lumitone postcard from its opening year, 1925. Its fourteen stories and five hundred rooms have accommodated the famous, like Henry Fonda and John F. Kennedy, as well as the infamous, such as the black bear that broke into the coffee shop in 1929. The card advertises amenities including a cocktail lounge and grill as well as golf and tennis in "the air conditioned city on beautiful Lake Superior."

Saulpaugh Hotel, Mankato, Minn. Traveling Men's Headquarters

In 1945, the year of this postcard, some hotels still catered to traveling salesmen, a vital occupation in the Victorian era later diminished by mail-order sales. Calling itself the "traveling men's headquarters," the Saulpaugh in southern Minnesota provided sample rooms where the vendor could display his goods for local retailers. This E. C. Kropp linen card advertises the majestic building, a Mankato landmark since 1894.

Room at the Inn

The lodging industry has always been an enthusiastic client of the postcard industry. Among Twin Cities business views, the most common is the hotel or motel card. Like resorts, hotels and motels enjoy the perfect combination of elements: a registration or writing desk at which to distribute free cards, the tourist's natural desire to write upon arrival at a destination, and the instinctive impulse to pick up a souvenir. In return, the hotel or motel gets free advertising transported all over the world.

THE RYAN HOTEL, ST. PAUL, MINN.

The Ryan Hotel, St. Paul, Minn.

Named after Dennis Ryan, who financed the hotel in 1885, the Ryan was a Victorian Gothic landmark loved by many until it was demolished in 1962. This Wright, Barrett, and Stillwell postcard is tinted to show the St. Paul building's red brick and bands of white Ohio sandstone. A luxury hotel, the Ryan had 335 sleeping apartments ranging in size from one to six rooms, one hundred with private baths.

Hotel Minnesotan, Minneapolis, Minnesota

Less fancy than the Ryan Hotel, this basic bedroom facility at 122–126 Washington Avenue South advertised itself in 1944 as "the best hotel value in Minneapolis," with rates starting at $1.50. The Curt Teich Company printed this card in 1944, the Hotel Minnesotan's opening year. The Panther Room, café, barber shop, and valet service all closed with the hotel in 1961, making way for a new building at Washington and Second.

HOTEL MINNESOTAN
Minneapolis' Newest Loop Hotel

MINNEAPOLIS
MINNESOTA

THE MINNESOTAN HOTEL FIREPROOF

VIEW OF LOBBY

THE PANTHER ROOM

Bill's Mount Silver Motel and Cabins

"Sleep to the Slap of the Waves" is the slogan for the Mount Silver Motel, perched on the shore of Lake Superior near Two Harbors. Offering the barest essentials, the motel's owner, William Nauha, advertised "Coffee – Lounge – TV." This minimalist approach is reflected in the simple photograph published as a chrome postcard in 1958 by Gallagher's Studio of Duluth.

Tourist Hotel, Grand Marais, Minn.

In the early days of Minnesota tourism, this hotel near the shore of Lake Superior depicted itself in a somewhat wild setting, with a man in the foreground holding a bear cub. Built as a boarding house and later moved across town to Wisconsin Street and First Avenue in Grand Marais, the Hotel Paine served visitors who ventured to the far northeastern tip of the state from about 1910 until 1926, when it burned to the ground.

Flour Power

During the peak years of postcard popularity, 1900–1915, Minnesota was recognized as "the miller to the world." No wonder, then, that dozens of milling postcards were published in the state. By 1900, there were 377 flour mills in Minnesota. Some, like the small Chaska mill, might produce only seventy-five barrels of flour per day, while their bigger brothers, the Pillsbury and Washburn mills in Minneapolis, each produced over 25,000 barrels per day. Local mills located on rail lines and near wheat fields prospered until the 1920s, when many were purchased by large milling companies. During the height of their prosperity, they took great pride in their brands, devising creative names and advertising them on flour sacks, postcards, and trade cards.

Although differing greatly in size and capacity, all of these mills were roller mills, grinding wheat into flour with a system of rollers instead of the traditional millstones. Because rollers made finer, whiter flour and yielded more flour from less wheat, the process was quickly adopted after it appeared in the 1870s. Minnesota millers had a lot to celebrate, and they advertised their processes and products on a multitude of postcards.

Minneapolis Milling District

During its prime, the west side milling district included the Palisade Mill, shown in the center of this card, and the Washburn-Crosby elevator number one, advertising the Gold Medal Flour brand on the left. More Minneapolis mills existed further left of this view. The rail lines in the foreground, used by a variety of companies, carried the milled flour to the Great Lakes and Atlantic Ocean for shipping all over the world. The photograph for this 1915 Acmegraph card, showing a bustling, productive city, was taken by C. J. Hibbard from another elevator, probably that of the Chicago, Milwaukee, and St. Paul Railroad at Second and Eighth.

St. Anthony Falls and part of Milling District, Minneapolis, Minn.

Louis Sweet took this multifaceted view of St. Anthony Falls in 1904, and R. Steinman published it as a white-border postcard around 1915. Behind the falls are the Stone Arch Bridge, a train leaving the Milwaukee Road depot, a row of mills, and the city courthouse tower. Steinman enhanced the bustling Minneapolis cityscape by adding smoke above the train engine and lights in the windows of the Northwest Consolidated A Mill.

St. Anthony Falls and part of Milling District, Minneapolis, Minn.

SLEEPY EYE MILLS.
WHERE SLEEPY EYE FLOUR IS MANUFACTURED—THE FINEST MILLING PLANT IN THE WORLD.

Sleepy Eye Mills

The mill in Sleepy Eye, Minnesota, advertised its "finest milling plant in the world" with a series of nine collectible postcards featuring Chief Sleepy Eye, a Sisseton Dakota considered "friendly" to whites. The enterprise's eight buildings produced 4,250 barrels of flour and feed per day in 1906, the year this card was published by Wilmanns Brothers of Milwaukee.

1887 — W. J. Jennison Milling Co., Appleton, Minn.
Elevator Capacity — 140000 Bus. daily
Mill Capacty — 700 Bbls. daily.

W. J. Jennison Milling Co., Appleton, Minn.

The Pomme de Terre River powered the W. J. Jennison roller mill in western Minnesota and provided a wonderful mirror for the stately structure rebuilt after a fire in 1905. Established in Appleton by Willis J. Jennison in 1896, the company produced millions of barrels of flour from 1906 to 1963. This St. Paul Souvenir Company card was sent in 1912 from a Railroad Post Office (RPO) on the Minneapolis and Osage Railroad.

Daniel Webster Flour

In around 1910, New Ulm's Eagle Roller Mill named its new flour for the American statesman Daniel Webster. Incorporated in 1892, the mill was producing five thousand barrels per day by 1906 and continued milling until 1953. The confidence expressed on the front of this postcard is reflected on the reverse side, where the company challenges customers to use the entire bag of flour, returning the empty sack to the dealer for a full refund if the flour does not produce "the best bread you ever baked."

MADE FROM DANIEL WEBSTER FLOUR

He wont be happy till he gets it

The Chaska farmers raise the wheat
That makes the flour, that can't be beat.
White Diamond is the name, "I wo't"
That's given it by Miller Scott.

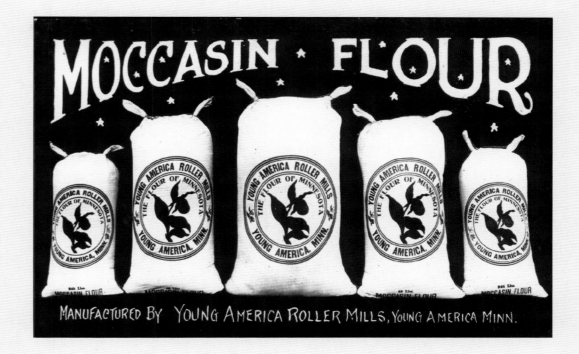

MANUFACTURED BY YOUNG AMERICA ROLLER MILLS, YOUNG AMERICA MINN.

Moccasin Flour

The Young America Roller Mills Company, operating just west of Minneapolis, preprinted the back of this circa 1910 real-photo postcard to wish customers a Merry Christmas. The greeting was also an opportunity to advertise Moccasin Flour, its name a pun on the state flower, the moccasin or lady's-slipper. Customers could buy their flour in bags weighing 24½, 49, or 98 pounds. The sender of this card added, "This is the kind of flour I use to bake my lovely daily bread."

White Diamond Flour

The woman on this 1908 postcard gained the viewer's attention by modeling a dress that no farmer's wife would have worn. It wasn't until the 1930s that flour sacks were recycled into clothing. W. H. Scott, owner of the Chaska Flouring Mill Company, hired the O. H. Peck publishing company to create this eye-catching card advertising its White Diamond Flour.

FLOUR MILL.   12. - CROOKSTON, Minn,

HANDCOLORED

Flour Mill, Crookston, Minn.

Four hundred barrels of Cremo Flour could be produced daily by Crookston's new electrically operated flour and feed mill, illustrated on this 1908 postcard lithographed and hand colored in France. The farmers sold their wheat and feed grain to the mill, which shipped the resulting flour by rail to the Great Lakes and worldwide, like the Minneapolis mills but on a smaller scale. The sender wrote, "Dear Wife and Baby, I reached here OK this morning. I have about a week's work I think. My material has not showed up yet. Good bye love, your husband."

Roller Mills, Lester Prairie, Minn.

"Lester Prairie Best" flour was produced at this mill, owned by the Newstrom Milling Company. The mill produced its first flour in 1890 and reached a top capacity of eighty-five barrels per day in 1917. The Cook Montgomery Company of Minneapolis published this real-photo postcard around 1915.

ROLLER MILLS LESTER PRAIRIE MINN.

Dear Madam, Bannons

An invitation to discomfort, this card was sent in 1941 to Florence Swain of St. Paul by Bannons Department Store. At the time, all women wore corsets—with rubber insets and heavy twill panels down the front for an "Even-Pul" or a "Flat Effect"—when going out in public. Without the help of Gertrude Schaeffer and her powerful devices, thousands of ladies might otherwise have been "loose" women.

American Wildlife Art Galleries

Artist Les Kouba, left, created and sold thousands of wildlife scenes during a career that spanned nearly five decades, from 1950 to 1998. Shown in a 1960s chrome card made by local photographer R. Meline, the American Wildlife Art Gallery in downtown Minneapolis's Plymouth Building sold prints and original works by Kouba and others. Kouba described himself as "52% businessman and 48% artist." The ad copy from the card's back underscores Kouba's formula: "you'll get untold hours of enjoyment and the satisfaction of having made a sound monetary investment."

Customers Wanted

Most postcards featuring a business were commissioned to advertise that business, usually with details included in the caption. But some cards blatantly promote a product or service, with preprinted advertisements on their reverse side. From artworks to dairy cattle, a little postcard can make the sale.

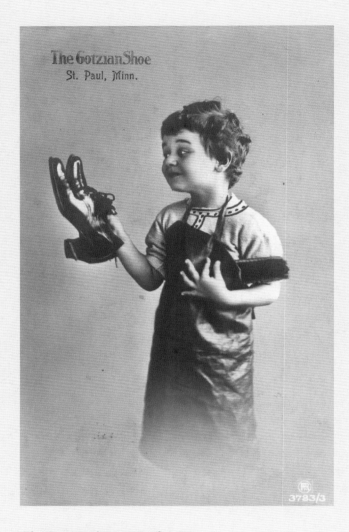

The Gotzian Shoe
St. Paul, Minn.

3783/3

The Gotzian Little Indian is Everywhere Because he is

"On the Trail of a Good thing" and so are You.

I will see you about

Still "Fits Like Your Foot Print".

Wonderland, Twin City Amusement Park, Minneapolis, St. Paul

Visitors to Wonderland found truly marvelous attractions. Opened in 1905 by the Twin City Wonderland Company, the amusement park on East Lake Street and Thirty-first Avenue South offered a scenic railway (roller coaster), airship swing, shooting the chutes ride, band concerts, and babies in incubators. This latter feature actually saved the lives of some premature babies for whom the hospitals did not have adequate facilities. In spite of its popularity, the park closed in 1911, unable to compete with amusement parks located on Lake Minnetonka and White Bear Lake. The lithographer of this card, Gustav Monasch of Minneapolis, also published this view as a gorgeous poster.

The Gotzian Shoe, St. Paul, Minn.

A traveling salesman's announcement card, this 1910 postcard bears on its back the trademark graphic of the Gotzian Little Indian and the company's slogan, "Fits Like Your Foot Print." In 1855 Conrad Gotzian founded the company that eventually manufactured and marketed shoes of all kinds from its huge plant at Fifth and Wacouta Streets in St. Paul.

MINNEAPOLIS WONDERLAND ST. PAUL

TWIN CITY AMUSEMENT PARK

Miss Minne Sota

What better way to lure settlers to southeastern Minnesota than with Miss Minne Sota, whose attire of local grains and grasses promised bounty and prosperity? Stella Gould, Dodge Center's studio photographer, created this real-photo card for real estate agent John Griswold in 1907.

P. W. Jensen, Deerhill Stock Farm, Millaca, Minn.

Straightforward and simple, this real-photo card shows the strength of Milaca cattle breeder Peter Jensen's stock. In 1912 he hired photographer E. L. Clement to make a card featuring his prize Holstein-Friesian bull, descended, as one might expect, from cattle of northern Germany's Holstein area bred with cattle from the Netherlands' Friesland.

Made from S. E. Minnesota grains and grasses in the real estate office of J. L. GRISWOLD, Dodge Center, Minn.

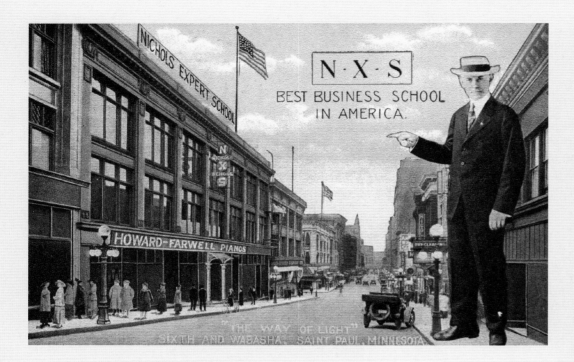

NXS, Best Business School in America

The giant man pointing proudly to the Nichols Expert School on Sixth and Wabasha in St. Paul is founder Malcolm Emery Nichols. In 1906 the school moved into its new ten-thousand-square-foot space filled with custom-designed furniture where it offered courses in all skills needed to be a first-class secretary or court reporter. This 1910 postcard by the R. Steinman Company includes the preprinted advertisement: "The NXS sells its catalog for 10 cents and redeems it for a dollar. I like its slogan—Business from start to finish." The school operated in this location until 1940, when Mr. Nichols retired.

Treasure Island Casino

The Cartwheel Company of St. Paul published this card for Treasure Island Casino, located on the Mississippi River near Hastings and operated by the Prairie Island Mdewakanton Dakota Indian Community. Established in 1984 as Treasure Island Bingo, the expanded casino's theme evokes the tropics, a locale especially appealing to Minnesotans trying to make it through the next long winter.

Ba! Ba! Black Sheep, have you any
wool?
"Yes, Kind Mistress, many bags
full:
Shear all the wooly flock, for shear-
ing never hurts,
And save the finest of the wool
to make "M" Shirts."

Minneapolis Knitting Works

"Expressed dress this afternoon, look for it. If not satisfactory, send it back. Let me know when you received it. We are all well hope you are better. Time is short, will write later," promised the sender of this card from Sioux Falls, South Dakota, in 1912. She used an advertising card for her message, one distributed by the Minneapolis Knitting Works Company, located at 620–708 Bryant Avenue North in Minneapolis and the cross-town competitor of the Munsingwear Company.

Minneapolis, Minn., 4/9 191 5

We have shipped your order by Omaha

frt and same

should reach you promptly. If any delay

in arrival, please advise and we will trace

shipment. Should you have occasion to

refer to this order, please mention num-

ber 13644

Yours truly,

Northrup, King & Co., Seedsmen.

Northrup, King & Co.'s Giant Marguerite Carnations

Located in Northeast Minneapolis from 1884 to 1985, the Northrup, King & Co. seed and flower distributor was a giant among Minnesota industries. During the golden age of postcards, the company used beautiful graphics to remind customers that their shipment was on the way.

Railroad Greetings

Two railroads headquartered in Minnesota—the Great Northern and the Northern Pacific—distributed postcards advertising the glories of railroad travel: smooth rides, classy interiors, personal services, good food, and picturesque scenery. Beautifully designed, the cards inspired passengers to write and recipients to travel.

"Limited" trains, like the North Coast Limited and the Oriental Limited, catered to first-class passengers. Designers tried to evoke both the comfort of home and the coziness of a private club. The railroads did offer "tourist" (second-class) tickets, but that service was not emphasized in advertising. The North Coast Limited was inaugurated in 1900, followed five years later by the Oriental Limited, named by its owners James J. and Louis Hill to underscore the company's reach to the Pacific Ocean, where Great Northern ships continued on to the Far East. Both the Great Northern and the Northern Pacific connected to Chicago via the Burlington (Chicago, Burlington, and Quincy) Railroad, and both lines ran to Seattle and Portland, the Northern Pacific slightly south of its competitor. For their postcard designs, the two competing companies hired talented photographers and outstanding illustrators to portray luxury and adventure.

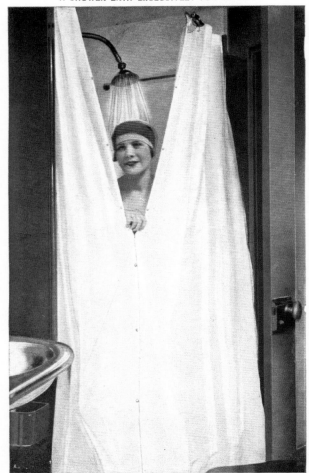

A Shower Bath Exclusively for Women

The caption for this 1920s view published by the Great Northern Railroad announces, "The modern and up-to-date woman has added to her repertoire of hygienic features and her daily toilette is no longer complete without the refreshing 'shower' bath." This E. C. Kropp card promotes modern conveniences offered to first-class passengers.

COMPLETELY EQUIPPED BARBER SHOP,
NEW ORIENTAL LIMITED.
GREAT NORTHERN RAILWAY

Barber Shop on the New Oriental Limited, Great Northern

The "new" Oriental Limited of 1924 offered many services, including a barber. After her hair was bobbed, this young woman could wander into one of the other first-class cars and read in the library or have a manicure. The barber also served as a valet and could do her ironing for her. Such personal touches helped popularize cross-country travel on the Great Northern Railway.

"Like Sterling on Silver," Northern Pacific Railway

For three days and two nights, riding from St. Paul to Tacoma, Washington, the Northern Pacific passenger of the 1920s was richly served. During this prime era of railroad travel, the scenery of North Dakota's Bad Lands, Montana's Rockies, and Washington's Yakima Valley passed by while the traveler feasted on fabulous meals, including the railroad's signature item, "the great big baked potato." The steaming trains on this 1913 card evoke speed, while the slogan "sterling on silver" connotes luxury and a smooth ride.

North Coast Limited in Bozeman Pass, Montana, Northern Pacific Railway

Artists sketched trains passing through scenic landscapes to advertise the breathtaking views from the Northern Pacific's rail cars. The commissioned art, some of it by Brown & Bigelow, was used on a variety of items, from postcards to menus and timetables to posters. Curt Teich probably printed this linen card in the 1950s.

"Traveller's Rest," Northern Pacific Railway

Raymond Loewy, famous modernist designer of streamlined objects, imposed his style on this North Coast Limited Buffet-Lounge car. According to the caption on the back of this 1960s card, "this crack transcontinental streamliner" also offered "stewardess-nurse service" and, judging from the front, a complimentary historical lecture on Lewis and Clark, whose campsite "Traveller's Rest" inspired the car's name.

"Traveller's Rest" for which this de luxe car was named, was a favorite campsite of explorers Lewis and Clark

CHAPTER THREE

The Personals

This is Paul, Lucy and Billie. Donald didn't happen to be at home so was not 'in it.' It is the best of Lucy for she is always laughing.

Card sent from Plainview, 1910

Some families are amazed to find an ancestor's portrait on a postcard because they think of cards as mass-produced items for tourists. But early in postcard history, in 1902, photo supply manufacturers like Kodak made producing real-photo postcards very easy. Their photo paper was made in standard 3½-by-5½ postcard size and weight with "Post Card" printed on the back. Anyone, including great-grandpa, could take the paper into a darkroom, expose it against a negative, and—presto!—produce a real-photo postcard. Many people, however, chose to have their postcards printed by the local photographer, who already owned a darkroom. This photographer also supplied the town with real-photo postcard views of its buildings, disasters, and festivals.

The opportunity to take and make personal postcards was pursued enthusiastically until about 1930, after which customers of the local photography studio preferred new types of portrait presentation, such as elaborate folders, instead of the handy little card. Today, it is still possible to make your own real-photo postcards with ordinary photo chemicals and postcard photo paper. Some prefer to select a favorite snapshot and affix it to an adhesive postcard back. Either way, the tradition of putting great-grandma on a postcard endures.

The Local Studio

From 1900 to 1930, most towns of a thousand or more citizens had a studio photographer who offered portraiture printed on a postcard. Some ambitious artists also offered

Mr. and Mrs. Walter Peterson and family

The twelve-foot skylight illuminating the Peterson family as well as the backdrop and the furniture around them have all been preserved as the Gust Akerlund Photography Studio at the Cokato Museum in central Minnesota.

Photographer's Studio Register

A page from Akerlund's 1909 business register lists "PCard" as the most common type of photograph ordered.

views of the town and the countryside. In Minnesota, one such studio survives: the Gust Akerlund Photography Studio, on display at the Cokato Museum.

When Signe and Walter Peterson, farmers from Stockholm Township near Cokato, brought their three children, Orville, Elda, and Bedford, to the Akerlund studio in 1928, they were following in the footsteps of hundreds of Meeker County residents. Gust Akerlund came to Minnesota from Sweden in 1902, stopping in Merrill, Wisconsin, to learn the photographic trade. By 1905 he prospered enough to buy land at Fourth and Broadway in Cokato, move his studio building there, and construct a skylight facing north. Many Cokato citizens were of Scandinavian descent, and the Swedish-born photographer easily related to them.

Akerlund first recorded orders for postcard portraits in 1907, and by 1909 the majority of notes in his business ledger indicate postcard sales. In the 1920s, customers began to prefer larger portraits, framed in art deco cardboard folders with romantic style names like "Obedius" and "Bagdad." But they continued to order postcards well into the 1930s. Akerlund's studio closed upon his death in 1954 and was reopened as a museum in 1986.

Another real-photo postcard photographer, Ross Daniels of Pine City, Minnesota, prospered for a shorter period than Akerlund amidst a very different clientele. Whereas Akerlund was surrounded by Swedes, Daniels's neighbors and clients included members of the Mille Lacs band of Ojibwe. Upon opening his business in 1910, he began making studio portraits of local Indians, probably at their request and not for the tourist trade. Later he printed and captioned postcards of native homes to sell to area visitors.

Although Kodak's product line enabled amateurs to take and make their own real-photo postcards as early as 1902, a town's photographer was the most prolific maker of such cards during the golden age. He or she recorded families and townscapes until the postcard craze diminished and other formats and larger companies took over the work.

Views of Work Life

Many real-photo cards featured occupations common in the first quarter of the twentieth century: men at work in the lumber and farming industries, women laboring at home or in the classroom. The personal message on the card often brings these scenes to life as, for example, one might imagine lumberjacks' cold hands penning greetings to friends back home. The correspondence from farmers and their wives typically reports on crops and the threshing season and occasionally conducts business. Mrs. Lillien Postell of Minneapolis received an apologetic notice from a farmer in 1906: "I had some chickens redy [sic] for you this morn but the dog bit them up so bad I was ashamed to send them. So I'll bring some alive when I come . . . got to help the folks trash [thresh] yet."

Some workers had to leave home to find a job. When they wrote to friends and family members, they portrayed a life of long hours and loneliness. Irene apologized via postcard to her friend Lillie in 1909 for not writing: "when I am working in the resturant [sic] I do not get much time as I work from 6 AM till 10PM." Similarly, that same year

Ross Daniels in his studio, Pine City, ca. 1910

Photographer Ross Daniels stands to the side in this image, making his studio, complete with postcards cluttering his desk, the central focus.

Hugo described his position in a flour mill to his friend George: "I am still alive, but I won't be if I keep on working in this place much longer. I work from 9PM to 7AM and it is pretty darn lonely. . . . How is Stella geting [sic] along?" One grim card, also from 1909, reports, "This is the place that John E. Nordin got killed," a matter-of-fact remark on dangerous working conditions, in this case at the Watab Paper Company and Mills in Sartell.

Messages from Family and Friends

The brevity imposed by the dimensions of a postcard makes it a perfect medium for flirting, teasing, and innuendo, as in the 1909 note from "Twinie" in Willmar to Jane

in Spicer: "Say, you should have been here yesterday, threshers fine! Ahem! One just fine for you."

Mass-produced cards change from the broadly public to the intimate once they are written upon and sent, but studio and homemade real-photo postcards begin and end on a personal level. Their messages stimulate our imagination to speculate about circumstances surrounding suggestive comments, as when S. M. Stephens wrote to Clara, "I am wondering about you. Let me know when you hear. . . . It seems like such a long time since I saw you. I got along beautifully this time. Am so glad it is out. . . . With love." Today's reader can't help but wonder what "it" was. If the card is in a family collection, the event may be explained by family lore, but postcards purchased at a sale dangle tantalizing hints of a story we will never know.

In the late nineteenth century, decorous people were concerned about the openness of postcard communication. G. W. Green wrote in *Atlantic Monthly,* "My grudge against the postal card is the tendency to read, against your own will, postal cards not addressed to yourself. There is a fascination about the thing which is very like kleptomania." But postcard writers knew their words were fair game for everyone, so they hinted at feelings by their choice in scene—comic or romantic—and made oblique references to events that only the recipient would understand. In a nod to the "danger" posed by postcard innuendo, Oswald

wrote to Mable in 1908, "Received your pretty postal some time ago. I burned the envelope. But forgot to leave the postal in so now it is in my album and I do not want to burn the album. If you do not like that I did not burn it you can burn my picture in place."

A series of postcards tells a story in the way a solitary note with veiled references cannot. Leon Bourque was employed by the Soo Line Railroad when he developed a yen for Polly Branchaud of Pembina, North Dakota. From 1909 to 1910 and from various spots along the rail line, he courted her with a combination of real-photo and lithographed postcards, their messages revealing his personality. His playful expressions portray an eager and sweet romantic: "I have been thinking so much of you today that I guess I will have to talk to myself," he writes on the day of his sister's wedding. Many of the cards appear to be written shortly after a visit, letting Polly know that he arrived home safely, "dreaming of you all the way." One card in particular provides a picture of his life and humor: "Hello Polly dear. I got home OK but it was no fault of the mosquitoes as they were so thick that I could catch them by the hands full. . . . I was wondering how the girls ever made it. I took off my hat and put the lap robe over my head. . . . Bye bye to the best girl for me in all the world. Leon." The card he chose for this message is an exaggerated tall-tale card; perhaps his note is an attempt at a small tale to make Polly laugh. Polly and

Leon were eventually married, according to the descendent who donated the sixty-five postcards to the Minnesota Historical Society.

Both sides of real-photo postcards deliver a glimpse into past lives. Made in small quantities, they usually carry a visual and personal message of work, home, or love, offering endlessly fascinating hints of stories we will never fully know.

Boiling cans, Canning Factory, Lyle, Minn.

During the fall canning season of 1911, a worker in Lyle, Minnesota, wrote to his friend in Bellingham, Washington: "Hello, How are you I am fine and dandy. Much oblidge [sic] for the card you sent me. We have been having fine weather here this week. I am still on the section with the dagoes Ha Ha. Greet them all from us all. Bye bye J. M. J. Greet all the girls from me Ha Ha." Local photographer George P. Anderson made postcards of this factory both inside and out.

Sawing logs

The sound of a crosscut saw was a daily companion for these lumberjacks, who were in the woods from Christmas until spring thaw. Early in the twentieth century, Bemidji photographer A. A. Richardson visited lumber camps to sell these men postcards of themselves at work.

Pride of Work

Throughout the golden age of postcards, occupational cards were common, produced not to advertise a business but to enable workers to proudly depict their work while sending a quick message to family and friends. During this period, many people replenished family coffers by working far from home, and postcards were the least expensive means of keeping in touch.

Farm near Akeley

This fall haying scene was sent from Akeley, Minnesota, to Wadena, Minnesota, with the message, "Dear Isaac. I will be home on Saturday if nothing happens, your wife Sarah." Rural communication took place via postcard rather than telephone or telegram until about 1915.

Woman at baking table

Women's work is infrequently shown on postcards, but this 1909 kitchen view was made in southern Minnesota's Fillmore County. An amateur photographer may have found the subject rolling out her dinner rolls in the light of a nearby window and decided to record the scene for the family.

Ushers, Minnesota Theater, Minneapolis

Standing at attention, ready to usher as many as four thousand moviegoers to their seats, these thirty-five "army trained college boys" were employed by the Minnesota Theater, one of the nation's largest when it opened in 1928. Photographer J. H. Kammerdiener arranged the army on the lobby's grand marble "stairway to happiness." Never filled to capacity, the theater closed in 1958.

House construction, Lakefield

Revealing the anatomy of a Dutch Colonial house, this 1915 postcard captures carpenters at work in Lakefield, Minnesota. This style originated in Pennsylvania, where German or "Deutsch" settlers built homes with barn-like roofs.

Postman in car

Rural mail carrier Caesar Wilson of Dassel, Minnesota, poses with his Metz car, purchased in 1910 to replace the horse and buggy that previously conveyed him over his forty- to fifty-mile route. He later patented a device for switching to larger rear wheels, the better to control his car in snowy conditions. When he retired in 1947, the local paper reported that he had driven more than 500,000 miles in the course of his career.

Twenty-fifth wedding anniversary card

Happy Anniversary! Mr. and Mrs. Rosener of Goodhue, Minnesota, deserve a celebratory card after twenty-three years of marriage and twenty-five children. This card, made for them in August 1908 by Frank Sjoblom, pictured them and their seventeen surviving sons and daughters.

Portraits

From 1905 to 1915, thousands of family portraits were printed on postcards. All photographers could produce them, no matter how small their studio or home darkroom. Every family collection has at least one.

Lillian Brown and Lauren

An archetypal home portrait: a mother embraces her son as she sits by the sewing machine. What became of Lillian and Lauren Brown after this 1910 photo? In this case, it's no mystery: she served as matron for the Albert Lea police department and he grew up to be a musician.

Bonnie and Dean Wilson and daughters

Surrounded by family pictures, Dean and Bonnie Wilson and daughters Nina (center right) and Annika (laughing) posed for their camera's self-timer. They printed the negative on postcard photo paper and sent it as their 1984 Christmas greeting.

Smoking cigars

Ross Daniels of Pine City, Minnesota, published marvelous real-photo postcards, including this self-portrait and tour-de-force in studio lighting, printed on AZO paper around 1915. Daniels is on the right, squeezing the shutter release as the fellow in the center lights his cigar.

Couple wearing hats

A stylish couple wears the latest finery, circa 1912. Her outfit mixes masculine shirt and tie with feminine accessories, evidence of women's growing presence in the business workplace. Bedecked in flowers, she may be having her picture taken for a special occasion, but what that might be we can only guess, as the back of the card carries no message.

Indian woman

An Ojibwe woman from the Lake Lena community poses in an automobile driver's fashionable attire. Ross Daniels, the photographer of this circa 1912 portrait printed on CYKO postcard paper, may have offered her the coat from his store of costumes, or she may be proudly displaying her own.

Indian man

This handsome Mille Lacs Ojibwe man posed for Ross Daniels in about 1913. He wears a dark shirt and pants to spotlight the beauty of his bandolier bags, belt, and moccasins, which may have been beaded by his wife, mother, sister, or aunt.

Charles A. Lindbergh and Dingo

Charles A. Lindbergh hugs his dog Dingo in a studio portrait made about 1914. Found on the family's doorstep in Little Falls, Dingo was young Charles's companion from 1912 to 1915.

Bragging Rights

The real-photo postcard, inexpensive and printed in small batches, provided the perfect medium for showing friends and relatives that the sender was successful and happy. An army of itinerant photographers met the demand for family photos, traveling with goat carts, donkeys, pedal cars, and other paraphernalia to entice proud parents of all economic classes. Even the author's father, who came from a humble carpenter's family, had a postcard portrait made of him and his brother on a pony. If there were no children to brag about, homeowners could feature their house or any other possessions they pleased.

Goat cart

Two boys pose in a goat cart near their St. Paul home circa 1910. Their parents paid about twenty-five cents to have this photograph made and printed, the slogan "Made in America," a confident declaration of their sons' bright futures.

St. Paul residence

Sara sent this postcard from St. Paul to White Bear Lake in 1910, proudly asking "How do you like our house and my hubby?" So that her friend could find her easily when she came visiting, she penned the house address on the steps and a further note on the back: "When you come to St. Paul, please don't forget me with a call."

Women from Kenyon

Pleased with both house and children, the women of 609 Front Street, Kenyon, Minnesota, called on local photographer Fred Borlaug to make a real-photo card in 1909. Mrs. Hannah Foss, seated in the center, wrote to her cousin in Glenwood, "the girl that is crossed [with an "x"] is mine, and baby walks everywhere already."

Santa Claus Air Line

Some families left home to pose in a particular locale. In this 1930s example, a department store Santa uses an airplane as a prop, advertising his up-to-date distribution system. The gifts he displays—Tinker Toys, dolls, and trucks—entice both boys and girls, and the number on the airplane links the photo to the customer.

Log barn

Instead of featuring his house, Oliver Juneau, a French Canadian railroad engineer, posed by a log barn built on forty acres near Rollins, Minnesota. His wife, Marie, and son, George, joined him on the right in this view taken around 1910.

Women and car

These two had reason to brag, and a postcard supplied just the opportunity. The driver, Dr. Gertrude Stanton, won the 1907 Oldsmobile in a Minneapolis newspaper popularity contest. She and daughter Sadie, riding in the back seat, were among Minnesota's earliest female optometrists.

CHAPTER FOUR

Our Vacation

Having heaps of fun. 75 fish before breakfast this morning.

Big Stone Lake, 1909

A trip without postcards is an incomplete journey. Postcards help us remember the sights we have seen and provide a tiny tablet on which to express our wit and personality as we communicate experiences and affection to friends and family. Minnesota has entertained multitudes of tourists through the years, and along the way its postcards have developed particular depictions of the state's lakes, forests, resorts, native inhabitants, and recreation. Subtly and quietly, postcards have shaped Minnesota's image.

Tourism in Minnesota

Minnesota's geographic sobriquet, "Land of 10,000 Lakes," describes a state made for postcard views. Since the earliest images of English seaside resorts and America's eastern shores, postcards have featured bodies of water as a central visual element. In Minnesota they can scarcely avoid it. Early views depicted lakes in the Twin Cities, with leisurely strollers and horse-drawn vehicles gracing the water's edge. Not far from the city lakes, popular resorts at Lake Minnetonka and amusements at White Bear Lake attracted postcard publishers as well as tourists. Then, shortly after World War I, people began to look to northern Minnesota for travel, rest, and recreation.

In her dissertation, *The Last Resort: Northern Minnesota Tourism and the Integration of Rural and Urban Worlds, 1900–1950,* Eileen Walsh describes the development of the state's resort industry. During the 1920s,

northern Minnesota's economy moved away from agriculture and lumbering and toward attracting tourists. Tourism in the state had modest beginnings: small roadside tourist camps or farmers providing accommodations for the occasional hunting or fishing group. But independent resort owners soon established businesses run somewhat like family farms, with everyone working, day and night, to provide an income to maintain the family's lifestyle. Log cabins and lodges became the symbol of the outdoor life and influenced the look of the businesses that supported that life. In 1961, a state survey found that 92 percent of all employment in thirty-four northern Minnesota counties was in resorts. By 1991, tourism ranked as Minnesota's second largest industry in terms of jobs.

In the midst of Minnesota's tourism boom, two postcard companies were established to help visitors and resort owners communicate the glories of a Minnesota vacation. William A. Fisher founded the W. A. Fisher Company of Virginia, Minnesota, in 1922, and Northern Minnesota Novelties (NMN) of Crosslake, Minnesota, began selling postcards in 1938.

A multifaceted printing company, W. A. Fisher developed postcards as one of its main products. The earliest Fisher cards are black-and-white views of resorts, many of them photographed in great detail by Mr. Fisher himself. He saw that the resort industry could keep his printing presses busy, so he spent a lot of time in northern Minnesota, photographing and taking orders for black-and-white printed postcards. Whereas today's resort owner might request one or two views of the property, Fisher's customers purchased views of the dock, the beach, the main lodge, several cabins, and interiors of sleeping, recreation, and dining facilities. Such postcards are a superb record of the resort environment and its amenities in the 1930s and 1940s. The simplicity of the living quarters and recreational facilities contrast strikingly with the luxuries expected in many resorts today: chenille-covered beds and a shuffleboard court don't have quite the same draw for most twenty-first-century tourists.

William Fisher's son Earl joined the business in the 1950s, and soon the company began printing chrome cards. Earl visited over five hundred resorts in northern Minnesota, making pictures of the buildings and lakesides and taking orders for cards. Between customers he made scenic photographs for postcards to be sold from racks at resorts and tourist attractions. Every drugstore and tourist spot on the Iron Range and along the North Shore stocked W. A. Fisher cards at some time. The company continued to make and distribute postcards of resorts, regional businesses, and scenic views through the 1980s.

Lured by the very lakes that Fisher was photographing, Dick and Ella Schalow bought a small postcard busi-

ness in Crosslake, Minnesota, moving from the Twin Cities to the heart of fishing and boating country in 1958. The company they bought, Northern Minnesota Novelties, had been established in 1938 to distribute Curt Teich view cards. The Schalows quickly revamped the business. As Dick explains it, "After the first year, we found out we did all right fishing, but we didn't make any money. So we ended up making some changes." The modifications included expanding into novelties, hiring photographer/salesman David Nordgren to cover a larger region, and changing the name of the company to NMN. While Fisher covered hundreds of resorts and produced only a few scenic cards, NMN specialized in scenic postcards of the state's lakes and forests, only occasionally working for resorts. Each year since 1960, NMN has published sixty to one hundred new views, removing the ones that sell poorly. The best sellers, according to Dick, are of the state capitol, the Mississippi headwaters at Itasca, and Paul Bunyan, a fairly representative example of major draws to the state.

Messages from the Road

Tourists' postcard messages have become a cultural cliché. "Having a wonderful time, wish you were here" calls to mind a happy vacationer writing to a less fortunate friend back home. We accept the cliché because postcard messages are usually abbreviated travel tales. This typical message, sent from Park Rapids, Minnesota, to St. Louis, Missouri, in 1952, sums up several days of activities in one small space: "Stopped at Rochester Min Sat night. Sunday stop at Fort Snelling National Cementary [sic]. Russ took pictures . . . going to Canada tomorrow. Dad & Russ caught 6 lb fish first hour."

Beginning in the 1930s, as roads were being paved for greater access to burgeoning resorts and amusements, more and more postcard messages began reading like vacation road reports, with travelers mentioning miles covered and time spent driving. More people had cars, and their pride in the automobiles' performance was rivaled only by their delight in their fishing prowess. As one frenetic vacationer wrote, "Drove straight thru – took 12 hours, got here 10:30 AM Saturday. Cooled off – only caught 7 fish so far. Be seeing you."

But road improvement was not universal, as some messages convey: "Total Mileage today 308 miles. Entire sections around here very wet. . . . Met two N Jersey *gentlemen* on a one track mud road – detour – radiator to radiator, practically. Altho it was our track, they smoked until we consented to take the risk of turning out in the mud. We left them face to face with another car Ha! Ha!" (Austin, Minnesota, to Union Grove, Wisconsin, 1937).

Postcard vacation reports contain glimpses into the lives of travelers. A card sent to Alden, Minnesota, in 1940

summarizes the elements of a good vacation for the writer: "This is our cottage where we are having the most glorious rest and good things to eat and fine beach to go bathing twice a day. Boys are out for an all day fishing. Yesterday we drove to Brainerd. We drove 32 mi in an hour. If the mosquitos bite [too] bad we won't pick blueberries." Rest, food, and fishing top many a postcard writer's list of favorite activities, and this researcher was surprised to see how many people mention picking blueberries.

Some messages were written with great enthusiasm: "Are we having fun, Boy, oh, boy! We went on a hike before breakfast (some girls and I) and then made a fire and cooked breakfast" (Brainerd, Minnesota, to St. Paul, 1941). Others are grumpy: "Did not sleep a wink last night and was told that I had to go to this *dam* this evening with a crowd of picnicers. so will have to get up at 4AM to get to Superior" (Cloquet, Minnesota, to St. Paul, 1909). Or there was the unhappy Iowan who wrote from Tyler, Minnesota: "I sure don't like Minnesota land at all. It's just lakes and ponds and lowland."

Prior to the 1930s, vacation postcard messages describe a slow, sedentary experience, usually written from a single spot where the tourist settled in: "Am enjoying life at Big Stone Lake this week. We have a small cottage and two tents here and are having heaps of fun. 75 fish before breakfast this morning" (Ortonville, Minnesota, to Min-

neapolis, August 1909). Even though they portray a peaceful existence, some early messages exude excitement: "You would just love this wild and wooly country. We are miles away from everyone . . . we are having the time of our young lives and just living" (Mary to Aunt Susan, Tower, Minnesota, to St. Paul, 1912). While the details of the messages change over the years, vacationing Minnesotans still seek rest, relaxation, and a big string of fish.

Tourists and Native Americans

As Minnesota's tourists expanded their travels and their numbers, the postcard images of the state's Indian population evolved to meet different expectations. According to anthropologist and historian Patricia Albers, the change occurred during the 1920s, with a shift away from picturing Native Americans in their indigenous surroundings, at home or in town, going about their everyday activities in ordinary clothing. The newer images posed them in scenic surroundings or at Native American attractions wearing Plains Indian garb uncharacteristic of their customary attire.

Albers speculates that early tourists perceived Indians as a natural part of their up-north surroundings, more like vacation neighbors than curiosities. This view is reinforced by postcard messages sent from northern Minnesota. Arthur wrote to Mrs. Blomquist, Milaca to Fore-

Indian Camp, Pine County, Minn. Daniels Photo

Ross Daniels prepared this view for commercial postcard sales, in contrast to his studio portraits of Indians made at their request.

ston, in 1908, "This is the picture of the chief and his family up at the lake. Don't they look swell." Another writer says "I thought you would like to see an old familiar face [John LeGard of Fond du Lac] the station agent takes pictures, has a lot over at the depot" (Fond du Lac to Minneapolis, 1909). Not only is the subject of the card "familiar," the photographer is part of the local scene, not a distant publisher in Chicago.

Postcards by small-town photographer Ross Daniels of Pine City illustrate the casual, indigenous look that Albers notes on the early

Indian at Itasca State Park

A caretaker at the Mississippi Headwaters Museum, Ben Little Creek from Red Lake was for many years a summertime personage at the river's source. Drawing on his Indian heritage (sometimes emphasizing effect rather than accuracy), he sold postcards and Indian crafts and posed for snapshots costumed in an assortment of Indian headdresses.

Greetings from Marvelous Minnesota, "Land of 10,000 Lakes"

This chrome postcard printed by W. A. Fisher for Jocko's Clearwater Lodge and Outfitters represents all the stereotypes of Minnesota outdoor life, from rustic voyageurs to happy campers to camera-toting tourists.

cards. His views of Ojibwe scenes matched those encountered daily by townspeople and tourists alike. The Indians in these views are not wearing ceremonial clothing, just their everyday shirts and skirts. Of course, some cards made before 1920 were clearly posed for the tourist trade. A popular postcard subject, John Smith—the oldest living Ojibwe at the time—can be found on dozens of cards wearing all manner of clothing.

Postcard scenes of Native Americans began to shift from natural to contrived as tourism gained importance in the 1920s. Indian attractions such as pageants and trading posts were created to draw visitors to vacationland, and on postcards advertising these sites Indian men wore war bonnets and buckskins, neither garment the traditional attire of the Minnesota Ojibwe. The subjects were commonly posed in nature-as-beauty settings instead of places one might actually meet them. A few stock postcards tried to evoke indigenous surroundings, but they were usually generic scenes, labeled with a dozen different locations depending on where the card was sold.

Minnesota's Image

Postcards portray what visitors believe to be the essence of a state. Since the postcard business is market driven, the views that tourists buy become the visual symbols of the region. Plenty of Minnesotans do not fish or live in log structures on lakes, yet as tourism developed into a mammoth business the lives of all Minnesotans increasingly came to be represented by a few common symbols.

After 1920, the imagery on Minnesota postcards highlighted the

beauty and amenities of northern Minnesota, emphasizing nature and buildings designed to fit their surroundings. Few cards featured the rich farmlands of southern Minnesota, though the occasional cow strays onto a card in contrast to the more popular deer and wolf. Select clichés are offered: the state's lakes and rivers appear to be created for the amusement of boaters and fishermen; tourist accommodations are made of logs and furnished to look rustic and casual; the flora and fauna are gentled and groomed for the camera. The state's people and places are re-created in a visual language that most viewers understand is purely fiction and mostly fun.

In the late 1930s, cards appeared with maps and tiny cartoon drawings of tourist attractions, wildlife, and activities associated with the Land of 10,000 Lakes. Fifty years later, the symbols of Minnesota outdoor life are neatly arranged at a generic campsite beside a nondescript lake, with the state bird, the loon, benevolently watching over the scene.

Tourism keeps the postcard industry in business. In

Minnesota

This chrome postcard based on photographs by Paul Sundberg was published by Erickson Postcards and Souvenirs of Duluth in the 1990s.

turn, postcards serve travelers by creating the perfect view to keep or to send and offering a place to record one adventure before they hurry on to the next. The postcard view, however unreal, imprints Minnesota-ness on their minds.

10291

DELLWOOD CLUB HOUSE DOCK, WHITE BEAR LAKE, ST. PAUL, MINN.

COPYRIGHT 1906 BY T. W. INGERSOLL

Dellwood Club House Dock, White Bear Lake, St. Paul, Minn.

Located on the eastern side of the Twin Cities, Dellwood offered boat clubs, sailing regattas, and other popular diversions for St. Paul's wealthier residents. F. Scott Fitzgerald frequented the White Bear Yacht Club, also known as the Dellwood Club, beginning in 1909, around the time A. C. Bosselman and Company published this card.

Vista from Tower of Approach, Big Island Park, Lake Minnetonka, Minn.

Rising out of beautiful Lake Minnetonka, Big Island offered considerable recreation opportunities to vacationers, who from 1906 to 1911 arrived from town via the streetcars and ferryboats of the Twin City Rapid Transit Company. This card by New York's A. C. Bosselman and Company shows the park's grand entrance at the ferry docks. From here the visitor could stroll to the amusement park, the picnic grounds, or the music pavilion.

VISTA FROM TOWER OF APPROACH, BIG ISLAND PARK, LAKE MINNETONKA, MINN.

10302.

First Attractions

At the turn of the twentieth century, most Minnesota tourists stayed close to Minneapolis and St. Paul. During the golden age of postcards, the most popular recreation sites were city parks, Lake Minnetonka, and White Bear Lake. Trains and streetcars carried people from their city dwellings to these places of rest and relaxation. Day trips were common, but grand hotels and rustic cottages were available for longer stays. Many visitors also considered the state capitol building a must-see attraction.

BIRDS EYE VIEW OF LORING PARK, MINNEAPOLIS, MINN.

Bird's eye view of Loring Park, Minneapolis, Minn.

A peaceful haven in the center of the "City of Lakes," Loring Park is a short stroll from the busy downtown and home to one of Minneapolis's thirteen lakes. Although this 1905 Rotograph view is unpopulated, the park has always been a beehive of activity.

N7 Minnesota State Capitol, St. Paul, Minn.

Minnesota State Capitol, St. Paul, Minn.

The gleaming white, marble-covered Minnesota State Capitol has been popular with tourists since its completion in 1905. Postcard views of it, like this drawing published by S. Landsdorf and Company of New York, were available even before the Cass Gilbert–designed building was finished. This "advance image" shows a lawn fountain that never graduated from the architectural plans and omits the gold-leaf sculpture of a horse-drawn chariot that stands today over the main portico.

Great Northern Pike, a few 10 to 20 pounders from Pequot, Minn.

Ice fishing apparently yields frozen fish, if this 1915 real-photo postcard from Crow Wing County in north-central Minnesota is any indicator. Wearing winter coats and newsboy hats, the men display their catches without the aid of stringers, simply holding the fish like planks of lutefisk.

Catch of the Day

Fishing reports are among the most common messages posted from Minnesota. Visitors to the lake regions, near Brainerd, around Bemidji, or in the Boundary Waters, invariably inform the folks back home about the catch of the day. Some fishers get skunked, like Dale in 1943, "Fishing hasn't been so good. I've only caught one bullhead," but overall they are indomitable: "So far no fish, but we will be trying again," wrote Taby to her mother in 1965. Often, women vacationers write the postcards while the men are out fishing. In 1952, one shorebound wife reported, "had all the fish we could eat and starting to freeze them to bring home. All eating like pigs. Men left 6 this morning." But many join in the fun: "Babe and I have been out everyday . . . to catch a big musky that has been seen in their lake. Would the boys be surprised if we caught one," wrote Sinia, who also washed clothes that day as Babe did the ironing.

According to the Minnesota Department of Natural Resources, about one and a half million people fish Minnesota's lakes annually. Over the years, dozens of cards have displayed anglers with their catches, as the postcard industry helps publicize the state's fish tales.

At Roseau Lake, Roseau, Minn.

At Roseau Lake, Roseau, Minn.

Near the Canadian border, in Roseau, Minnesota, these dressed-for-church fishermen and -women posed for local photographer Olaf A. Holm in 1910. The card portrays fishing as an ageless and gender-neutral sport—and one that achieves spectacular results.

A fight with a mad Pickrel.

A fight with a mad Pickrel

William H. Martin of Ottawa, Kansas, created an exaggerated postcard by combining two or three photos and drawing on the negative so that fishermen could send a card about "the one that got away." Ivan, who sent this card to Clara in 1911, could not resist adding his own humor, writing, "I've been fishing for a bid to the Leap Year dance."

111

THE MINNESOTA FISHERMAN'S HIERARCHY OF FISH

1) Muskellunge
2) Walleye
3) Northern Pike
4) Largemouth Bass
5) Crappie
6) Sunfish
7) Skunked
8) Bullhead

Indian Beach Resort

This Kandi-Yo-Hi chrome postcard from the 1950s matches the tone of its subject: Green Lake. Located in central Minnesota and owned by Dave and Edythe Schmiedeker of Spicer, Indian Beach Resort offered sixteen cottages, a beautiful lagoon, and fish freezing facilities.

The Minnesota Fisherman's Hierarchy of Fish

Modern comic postcards such as this 1990s specimen by NMN of Crosslake play on a different aspect of fishing lore than the Martin cards. Except for the skunk, this portrayal of how Minnesota fishermen rate their catches is fairly accurate. The lowly bullhead was always the least desirable fish, until the discovery of the eelpout.

Barefoot boy and carp

This barefoot boy in a classic pose is James Taylor Dunn in about 1920, when "Jimmy," as he is named on the back of this real-photo card, was eight years old. After growing up along the St. Croix River, James became chief librarian at the Minnesota Historical Society.

American Point Resort, Most Northern Point in U.S., Penasse, Minn.

With a fisherman's slogan above her head, a female angler proudly displays her walleye in this 1950s real-photo card by the A. Pearson Company. At American Point Resort, a fishing guide could be hired for eight dollars a day, clearly a worthwhile investment. The resort was located on a fifty-one-acre island on Lake of the Woods, near a post office that could claim to be the United States' most northerly—until Alaska became a state in 1959.

Native Culture

Minnesota's vacationers met Native Americans in towns near reservations and at tourist attractions with adjoining gift shops up through the 1960s. The advent of the American Indian Movement drew the Indians back to their homes, while postcards began to more accurately illustrate their interests and culture.

Ojibwe family in Onamia, ca. 1910

Posing for an itinerant photographer named Smith, the Ojibwe family of Tom Weyaus took a moment from their visit to town to have a real-photo postcard made. Mom, Dad, and baby Ole lived on the Mille Lacs Indian reservation.

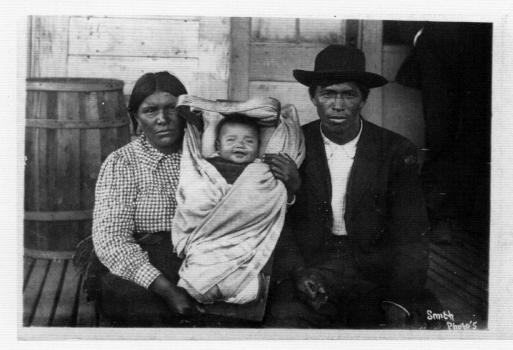

Cooking a meal, Mille Lacs, ca. 1920

Maggie Sam, a member of the Mille Lacs Ojibwe band, prepares food over an open fire. This real-photo postcard was likely made by Harry Ayer, owner of a trading post on Lake Mille Lacs. The natural scene differs greatly from later postcard images in which the subjects would be asked to wear uncharacteristic regalia.

Nick's Indian Gift Shop

Tourists passing Onamia on Highway 169 were attracted to Nick's Indian Gift Shop. Although located in the heart of the Mille Lacs Ojibwe reservation, the white block building was covered with Southwestern and Plains Indian symbols. Members of the Pewaush family posed in outfits supplied by Nick's for this circa 1956 L. L. Cook chrome card.

Hello from Aitkin, Minnesota

By the time this chrome card was published by G. R. Brown Company of Eau Claire, Wisconsin, in the 1960s, Native American portraits consisted of an unnamed generic object in an Indianlike setting. "Hello from" cards recycle images with different place names, like this one "from Aitkin," which was also used for Grand Portage and other northern Minnesota towns.

CASS LAKE MINN.

Not nearly as grand as some hotels on Lake Minnetonka, the Hotel Buena ▶
Vista on Cook's Bay near Mound nevertheless pleased the sender of this
A. C. Bosselman postcard in 1910. Peggy Flo wrote to Alice, "We are en-
joying this hotel very much. I have been having dandy fine times bathing,
launching, Lovers' Lane, marshmallow toasts, etc."

John Smith, age 128, Cass Lake, Minn.

Popularly known as John Smith, this Ojibwe man, Ka-be-na-gwe-wes, was a postcard
personality. Appearing on over forty different views, he often sold these postcards on
local trains traveling near Walker, Cass Lake, and Bemidji. Each card reports his age
somewhat differently, as his early-nineteenth-century birth date was not precisely
known. He died in 1922.

Mystic Lake Casino

In recent years, Native American groups have published their own
cards, displaying their culture as they prefer it to be seen. Showing
accurate traditional dress for Dakota on the left and Mandan-Hidatsa
on the right, this card is from Mystic Lake, a highly successful Indian
casino near Minneapolis.

Rustic Lodgings

Like postcards, resorts were created to fill a need. Customers needed to get away, and business owners needed an income while living in their chosen locale. The earliest resort-type businesses were lakeside hotels or farmhouses that provided a room for the night. When farming diminished as a viable activity in northern Minnesota, local residents built cabins and lodges for urban nature seekers who came by train and, increasingly, by car.

As the industry developed in the 1920s and '30s, rustic decor and ambiance became the norm. Big fireplaces, log furniture, and log walls made customers feel they had left their normal abodes for a place of relaxation close to nature. Of course, not all Minnesota resort cabins are totally rustic. For customers who wanted the comforts of home, resorts offered amenities like modern appliances and heating units. Then tourists began expecting entertainment facilities like recreation rooms and swimming pools. Nature receded, and elements of urban life became necessary attractions.

Pine Shores Resort Entrance on Mission Lake, Merrifield, Minn.

The archway to Pine Shores Resort, located near Lake Itasca, contains the key elements of Minnesota's developing resort industry: automobiles and roads, pines and shorelines. This real-photo card was made on Kodak postcard stock around 1939, the year of the Chevrolet "Master Deluxe" parked in the driveway.

Tourist camp

Before resorts and lodges were abundantly available, tourist camps were popular destinations. People hit the road and traveled cross-country or to the north woods for a taste of the outdoors. They slept in tents or in makeshift camping trailers and flocked to community facilities, like this one at Two Harbors' Rustic Inn, for shelter and travel-tale swapping. This real-photo postcard is from 1925.

The Wilkie House, Lake Pokegama, Pine City, Minn.

The first resorts were hotels perched on the edge of a lake, like the Wilkie House in Pine County, just west of Pine City. This circa 1907 view suggests at least two agreeable options for guests: sun-splashed days of fishing on Lake Pokegama or leisurely afternoons and evenings in the comfort of a screened-in porch.

Douglas Lodge, Itasca State Park, Minnesota

Located near the source of the Mississippi River, Douglas Lodge is one of the state's most popular retreats. Built in 1905 using pine logs from Itasca State Park, it has accommodated guests since 1911. This card by the Albertype Company of Brooklyn, New York, emphasizes the natural setting of the lodge and its surroundings on Lake Itasca. Its namesake, Wallace B. Douglas, was instrumental in preserving the majestic timber that distinguishes the park.

Dining room, Klose to Nature Kamp, Ten Mile Lake, Hackensack, Minn.

In 1921 Anna Marie Robertson purchased an island on Ten Mile Lake where she developed a resort that mixed bucolic and refined—her Klose to Nature Kamp. By surrounding dining-room guests with birch logs, stuffed birds, and wasp nests and serving meals on delicate china with fine linens, she helped them feel both rustic and genteel. The sender of this 1920s real-photo postcard commented, "Food great. . . . Fishing is good."

Gateway Lodge, Grand Marais, Minn.

Offering access to the Boundary Waters, Gateway Lodge was later known as Hungry Jack Lodge, located on Hungry Jack Lake in Superior National Forest. Owner Jesse Gapen built the first lodge in 1924, but this 1940 real-photo card shows the lodge rebuilt after a 1931 fire. Furnished with handmade pieces by local craftsmen, the new lodge was the largest log structure in the Midwest—126 by 64 feet.

Interior of cottage #8, Marvin's Modern Cottages on Lake Koronis, Paynesville, Minn.

A 1945 resort guide advertised what this real-photo postcard shows: Marvin's Modern Cottages had electric stoves, refrigerators, and an oil heater for spring and fall vacations, all for thirty-five dollars a week. In this "home away from home," the furniture and décor mirror what might be found in the permanent abodes of its temporary residents.

"Dusk," Ludlow's Island Lodge, Cook, Minn.

Like those at Marvin's, the cabins at Ludlow's Island Lodge contained the amenities and furniture styles of the 1940s middle-class home—but with knotty pine walls to suggest rustic surroundings. The resort opened on Lake Vermilion, near the Boundary Waters, in 1946, and W. A. Fisher printed this postcard soon after.

"DUSK" — LUDLOW'S ISLAND LODGE, COOK, MINN.

The Bar at Esslinger's Resort on Lake Kabetogama, Minn.

As the resort industry developed, customers demanded more recreational choices, especially when it came to evening entertainment. Esslinger's Resort on Lake Kabetogama kept guests occupied with a jukebox, a pinball machine, and a bar, as advertised in this circa 1950 L. L. Cook postcard. This image, made from an original postcard negative, includes details at the edges that would have been cropped out on the card.

Log cabin at Virginia Lodge, Sturgeon Lake, Minn.

The epitome of the small log-cabin resort, Virginia Lodge was located on Sand Lake in Pine County, about one hundred miles north of the Twin Cities. The Hamilton Postcard Company of Ames, Iowa, captured this real-photo view, which included a guest's 1949 Chevrolet "Fleetline."

Smokey Point Lodge on Big Leech Lake, Walker, Minn.

Typical Minnesota resort cabins, both white-sided and of log construction, face the south side of Leech Lake, one of Minnesota's largest. Advertised on the back of this 1930s Albertype postcard for Smokey Point Lodge are the amenities of birch and maple trees—a truly back-to-nature setting.

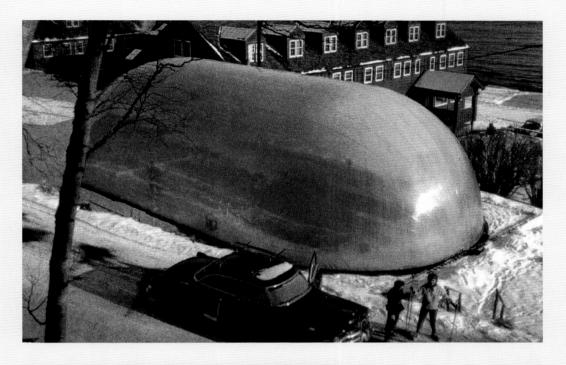

Lutsen Resort, Lutsen, Minn.

"Skiing on outside, swimming on inside"—as these 1959 Fisher chrome cards proclaim—were activities simultaneously available to Lutsen Resort guests thanks to a huge Mylar bubble made by the Sheldall Company of Northfield, Minnesota. Though this experimental cover lasted only a year, the Lake Superior resort has existed for more than one hundred. With the addition of a ski lift in 1948, Lutsen became the state's premier ski resort.

The NANIBOUJOU LODGE

The Naniboujou Lodge

Appropriately named with the wonderful word for a forest spirit, this fine lodge was built and decorated with Cree Indian motifs in 1928. Originally an exclusive club meant to attract famous members like Babe Ruth and Jack Dempsey, the Naniboujou Lodge is now open to anyone willing to travel to the North Shore near Grand Marais. This Cartwheel Company postcard features the dining room's magnificent two-hundred-ton stone fireplace—Minnesota's largest, earning the lodge a spot on the National Register of Historic Places.

Baking at Ruttgers Bay Lake Lodge, Deerwood, Minn.

Established by Joe and Josie Ruttger in 1898, Ruttger's on Bay Lake may have been northern Minnesota's first resort. Joe's initial plan was to farm forty acres, but his house turned into a resort when fishermen arriving by train needed a place to stay. Josie, a skilled cook, fed them well, and her tradition was carried on decades later by Bertha and Amy Pleidrup, pictured in this 1960s chrome postcard by L. L. Cook.

One Final Message

On the following page is my favorite postcard. It is part fact, part fiction, as all postcards are.

The facts that explain the origin of this card are visible on its front and back. Mrs. Bertha Kuchenbecker, a candy store owner in Detroit, Minnesota, contracted with Charles Morris of Chinook, Montana, to make a color postcard that would represent her region. Mr. Morris made a photograph depicting a fishing trip, which he sent to Germany to have printed in color. He delivered the finished cards to Mrs. Kuchenbecker, who was no doubt delighted to see her name printed in red on the card's front.

The back of the card includes a stamp box with Charles Morris's logo in it. It has a divided back, evidence that it was published after 1907. The writing indicates it was given to Wesley Hillier by his grandpa. It was either sent in an envelope or never mailed at all since there is no stamp, postmark, or cancellation. This golden age postcard was made when collecting cards was everyone's hobby, and Wesley may have slipped the card into his postcard album.

But a closer look at the photograph suggests that there is something fishy about this card. A postcard about great fishing in northern Minnesota, especially around Detroit, would typically have a lake in view. Detroit, now known as Detroit Lakes, boasts 412 lakes within a twenty-five-mile radius. Did these two men haul their catch to a grassy spot just to construct a fish tepee? Was the large wagon pulled by strong horses required to transport all those fish? How did the boat on the cart arrive at this place? And finally, why are these fishermen not dressed for fishing?

My suspicion is that this view is itself a fish story, manipulated by the publisher to tell a whopper. Charles Morris, known as the "cowboy photographer" of Montana, was famous for his documentary photographs of the west. After riding the range for thirteen years, he set up a studio

A Fish Tepee caught near Detroit, Minn.

A Fish Tepee caught near Detroit, Minn.

in Chinook, Montana, from which he published his own photographs as postcard views. His postcards are full of horses, wagons, cowboys, and tepees.

Among his many photographic talents, he was skilled at making tall-tale postcards. In this case, I think he merged details of several photographs to construct the ultimate fish story. The process, possible with copy photography and negative retouching, would have involved several steps. First he found a photo of fish displayed as a tepee, perhaps provided by Mrs. Kuchenbecker. Then he borrowed two men from some of his cowboy or fort photos,

evidenced by the Stetson hat and the military jacket, and lifted the horses from one of his scenes of Montana homesteaders. Against an unidentifiable background, he merged these disparate images in the darkroom. I haven't found these exact images in publications of his original photographs, so maybe this explanation is my tall tale. But I suspect I am close to the truth.

What did I learn by studying this postcard? The facts of its production: published between 1907 and 1910 by a talented guy from Montana, who had it printed in Germany and then sold it to a confectioner in Detroit to distribute in her store. The understanding of its use: a gift from grandfather to grandson. I also had the pleasure of reading about its maker in *True, Free Spirit: Charles E. Morris, Cowboy Photographer of the Old West,* a biography of Morris by his son, Bill, as I searched for facts to support my theory about its fabrication as a tall tale.

By looking closely at this "fish teepee caught near Detroit, Minnesota," I practiced my technique for discovering the stories each postcard may contain. Every postcard has a tale about creation and communication. To find the story, simply follow the clues.

The Postcard Makers

Most of these short descriptions were compiled from interviews and from city directories and biography files at the Minnesota Historical Society. The Minnesota scope notes were calculated from a 1996 survey of postcards in the Minnesota Historical Society collection. Information on Charles Morris came from his son, Bill, and Curt Teich facts from the Curt Teich Postcard Archives at the Lake County Discovery Museum, Wauconda, Illinois.

A. Pearson Company

Minneapolis
Business dates: 1906–1980
Type of business: postcard publisher and greeting card sales
Type of postcards: real photo
Owners: Founded as Pearson-Ullberg Company by Theodore Pearson and partner Gottfried Vallinder. Adolf Pearson bought out his brother in 1911 and ran the business until 1956. (In 1920, Adolf bought the Co-Mo Company, but he maintained ownership for only one year.) Adolf's son Everett led the business from 1956 to 1971, and Daniel, Gary, and Stephen Pearson continued the greeting card business until 1980.
Minnesota scope: 55 counties, Twin Cities
National scope: Minnesota, Iowa, North Dakota, South Dakota, Wisconsin

Gust Akerlund

Cokato
Business dates: 1902–1953
Type of business: portrait studio
Type of postcards: real photo
Owner: Gust Akerlund was born in Sweden in 1872 and became a U.S. citizen in 1900. He built his main studio in 1905 and worked out of it until his death in January 1954. The studio is on the National Register of Historic Places and open to visitors.
Minnesota scope: Cokato area

Bloom Brothers

Minneapolis
Business dates: 1907–1996
Type of business: postcard publisher (1907–1928) and novelty company
Type of postcards: black-and-white and color printed, frequently by Curt Teich; a few real-photo cards
Owners: Founded by Benjamin, Harry, and Moses Bloom in Minneapolis. Later owners included Barney Tremblatt, Morris J. Weinstein, Nathan S. Siegel, Samuel L. Bloom, Al Quello, and John W. Allen.
Minnesota scope: 57 counties, Twin Cities
National scope: Minnesota, North Dakota, South Dakota, Yellowstone Park

Cartwheel

St. Paul
Business dates: 1980–present
Type of business: postcards and souvenirs
Type of postcards: chrome
Owner: Photographer Jerry Stransky origi-

nally produced postcards for his commercial clients and then published and sold a variety of view postcards. Now most images on his cards are the work of other photographers.

Minnesota scope: 14 counties, Twin Cities
National scope: Minnesota, Wisconsin

Co-Mo Company

Minneapolis and Milwaukee
Business dates: 1917–1942
Type of business: postcard publisher
Type of postcards: real photo, color printed
Owners: Founded by Lloyd L. Cook and Harris P. Montgomery in Minneapolis. Also known as Cook Montgomery Co. and L. L. Cook Co. Cook moved most of the company to Milwaukee in 1920. That same year, Adolph Pearson took ownership of the company, but Montgomery resumed ownership in 1921. William H. Becken is listed as the owner in Minneapolis city directories beginning in 1931.
Minnesota scope: 54 counties, Twin Cities
National scope: Minnesota, Iowa, North Dakota, South Dakota, Wisconsin

Ross Daniels

Pine City
Business dates: ca. 1910–1925
Type of business: portrait studio
Type of postcards: real photo
Owner: Ross Daniels was born in 1885 in Harmony Township, Fillmore County, and his family moved to Pine City in 1910. He moved to Minneapolis with his parents in 1925 and worked for the Zintsmaster photo studio.
Minnesota scope: Pine County

Duluth Photo Engraving

Duluth
Business dates: 1914–1929
Type of business: engraving and pre-press work; published cards printed by Curt Teich
Type of postcards: black-and-white and color printed
Owner: Ray D. Handy was manager and engraver from 1914 to 1927. Located in the *Duluth Tribune* building, the company served the newspaper's engraving needs, and Handy was also a *Tribune* cartoonist. After 1929, Handy continued to distribute Curt Teich cards.
Minnesota scope: 4 counties

Erickson Post Cards and Souvenirs

Duluth
Business dates: 1978–present
Type of business: postcards and souvenirs
Type of postcards: chrome
Owner: Larry Erickson bought the business from Annabelle Gallagher of the Duluth Gallagher photo studio.
Minnesota scope: North Shore and Duluth
National scope: Minnesota, Wisconsin

V. O. Hammon

Minneapolis and Chicago
Business dates: 1904–1930s
Type of business: postcard publisher
Type of postcards: color printed

Owners: Founded by Victor O. Hammon in Minneapolis in 1904 and in Chicago in 1906. Hammon left Minneapolis in 1907–08 for Chicago and kept branch managers in Minneapolis until 1923.
Minnesota scope: 13 counties, Twin Cities
National scope: Minnesota, Illinois, and Michigan; Milwaukee, Wisconsin, and St. Louis, Missouri

E. C. Kropp

Milwaukee
Business dates: 1896–1956
Type of business: postcard publisher and printer
Type of postcards: color printed
Owners: Emil C. Kropp founded the company; Frederick M. Wilmanns became president after Kropp died in 1907. Company sold to Johnson Printing of Minneapolis in 1957.
Minnesota scope: 64 counties, Twin Cities
National scope: nationwide

L. L. Cook Company

Milwaukee
Business dates: 1911–1969
Type of business: postcard publisher and greeting card sales
Type of postcards: real photo, linen, and chrome
Owner: Founded by Lloyd L. Cook in Lake Mills, Wisconsin; he also founded the Co-Mo Company in Minneapolis in 1917. Printing plant established in Milwaukee in 1921. Merged with GAF, Inc., in 1969 and stopped selling postcards. Maintained photofinishing

business until 1980. Donated negatives of Minnesota images to the Minnesota Historical Society in 1967.

Minnesota scope: 50 counties, Twin Cities
National scope: nationwide, with an emphasis on the middle states and Florida

Lidberg

Red Wing
Business dates: photo studio opened in 1892; postcards produced ca. 1900–1915
Type of business: postcard publisher and photographer
Type of postcards: color printed
Owners: Studio founded by Anders Lidberg; run by son Edward during the postcard era.
Minnesota scope: Goodhue County

C. L. Merryman

Kerkhoven, with branches at Spicer and Sunburg
Business dates: 1892–1940
Type of business: photography studios
Type of postcards: real photo and printed; also panoramic postcards
Owner: Charles Lincoln Merryman, born in Bangor, Maine, came to Minnesota in 1892 and immediately set up a studio. His collection of prints, including many postcards, was donated to the Minnesota Historical Society.
Minnesota scope: Swift & Kandiyohi Counties

Charles E. Morris

Chinook and Great Falls (Mont.)
Business dates: in Chinook, 1903–1909

Type of business: In Chinook, photo studio and postcard publishing; in Great Falls, the Charles E. Morris Co. store sold postcards, stationery, and art supplies.
Type of postcards: black-and-white and color printed
Owner: Charles E. Morris
Minnesota scope: 4 counties
National scope: Minnesota, Montana

NMN

Crosslake
Business dates: 1958–present
Type of business: postcards and souvenirs
Type of postcards: chrome
Owner: The company was originally Northern Minnesota Novelties, owned by Richard Schalow with his wife, Ella, and son Tim. Another partner, Dave Nordgren, took many of the photographs. NMN uses a dating code: starting in 1960 with the letter "B," each succeeding year is a new letter, reaching "Z" in 1984 and starting over with "A" in 1985.
Minnesota scope: 30 counties, plus the Twin Cities and state parks
National scope: Minnesota, North Dakota, and Wisconsin

Paul Reichelt

St. Paul
Business dates: 1901–1920
Type of business: postcard publisher and bookseller
Type of postcards: black-and-white and color printed
Owner: Paul Reichelt may have been the first

to publish postcards of St. Paul. One of his cards is illustrated in the *St. Paul Dispatch* of January 4, 1908, described as "the first St. Paul postcard." His business was at 7 West Fourth Street and then at 70 West Seventh Street. The newspaper article refers to him as "the original postcard dealer in the city."
Minnesota scope: St. Paul

A. A. Richardson

Bemidji
Business dates: ca. 1907–1922
Type of business: commercial photography studio: A. A. Richardson Photo-Illus. Co.
Type of postcards: real photo
Owner: Arthur Allen Richardson owned and operated his Bemidji studio until he moved to Minneapolis in 1922. There he used the professional name "Rich." From his Bemidji studio he made many trips to lumber camps to photograph and then sell to the lumberjacks. He was also known for his panoramic photos, some of which were printed as folding postcards.
Minnesota scope: Beltrami and Polk Counties

St. Paul Souvenir Company

St. Paul
Business dates: 1908–1912
Type of business: postcards and novelties
Type of postcards: black-and-white and color printed; real photo
Owner: Conrad Hamm
Minnesota scope: 46 counties, Twin Cities
National scope: Minnesota, Iowa, Montana, North Dakota, South Dakota

Richard J. Steinman

St. Paul

Business dates: 1907–1945
Type of business: postcards and advertising novelties
Type of postcards: real photo and printed
Owner: Richard J. Steinman
Minnesota scope: 13 counties, Twin Cities

Curt Teich

Chicago

Business dates: 1898–1978
Type of business: postcard printing and publishing
Type of postcard: color printed and chrome

Owners: Curt Teich Sr. and Curt Teich Jr. Company sold in 1976 to Regensteiner Publishing.
Minnesota scope: 47 counties, Twin Cities
National scope: nationwide

W. A. Fisher Company

Virginia (Minn.)

Business dates: 1922–present
Type of business: commercial printing, including postcards
Type of postcards: black-and-white printed and chrome
Owners: Founded by William A. Fisher; his son Earl joined the business in 1953. In 1990 the company was purchased by local businessmen Mark Leese and Eric Norri.
Minnesota scope: northern Minnesota, Twin Cities
National scope: Minnesota, Wisconsin

Wright, Barrett, and Stillwell

St. Paul

Business dates: 1901–1913
Types of business: paper and stationery
Type of postcards: printed
Owners: Frederick P. Wright, Samuel E. Barrett, and Eugene J. Stillwell
Minnesota scope: 5 counties, Twin Cities

INDEX

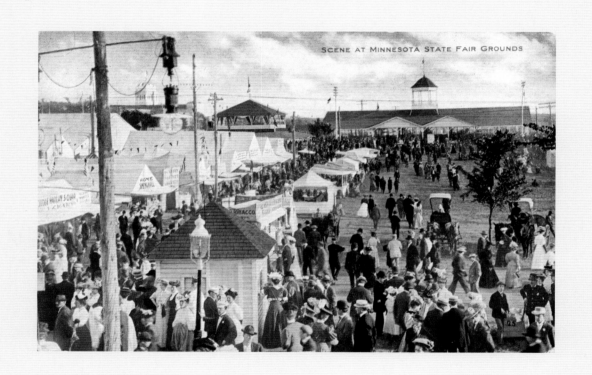

SCENE AT MINNESOTA STATE FAIR GROUNDS